Heirloom Rooms

Heirloom Rooms

SOULFUL STORIES OF HOME

ERIN NAPIER

With photography by Brooke Davis-Jefcoat

GALLERY BOOKS

New York   London   Toronto   Sydney   New Delhi

G

Gallery Books
An Imprint of Simon & Schuster, Inc.
1230 Avenue of the Americas
New York, NY 10020

First Gallery Books hardcover edition October 2023

GALLERY BOOKS and colophon are registered trademarks
of Simon & Schuster, Inc.

For information about special discounts for bulk purchases,
please contact Simon & Schuster Special Sales at 1-866-506-1949
or business@simonandschuster.com.

The Simon & Schuster Speakers Bureau can bring authors
to your live event. For more information or to book an event,
contact the Simon & Schuster Speakers Bureau at 1-866-248-3049
or visit our website at www.simonspeakers.com.

Interior design by Laura Palese

Manufactured in the United States of America

10 9 8 7 6 5 4 3 2 1

Library of Congress Control Number: 2022931838

ISBN 978-1-9821-9043-9
ISBN 978-1-9821-9044-6 (ebook)

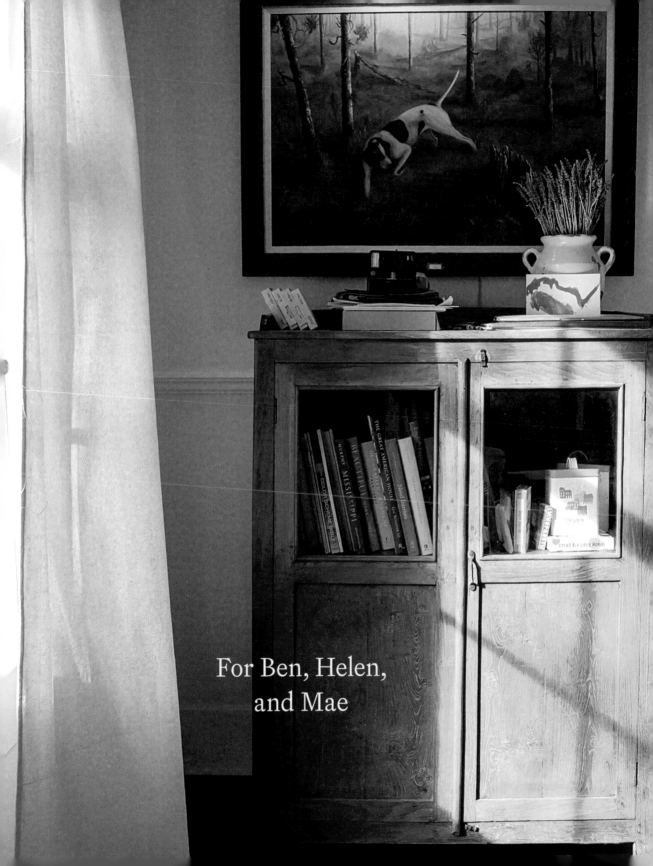

For Ben, Helen,
and Mae

Contents

Preface

THE HOME in Laurel, Mississippi, where my family lived when I was born was built by my grandfather James Rasberry in 1955. This is what I can remember about it: The beige marbled shag carpet in the den, where I have seen video of me in a Playskool car, babbling to my mama; this is where I lay on the floor watching *Pippi Longstocking* on VHS over and over. The almond and brown seashell-themed guest bath in the hallway, across from my bedroom. The sunken carport turned rec room off my brother's bedroom, where Clark played Ping-Pong with his friends, and I whined because they wouldn't let me play because I was nine years younger. I remember the light-blue chenille bedspread that covered me on my parents' bed, where I slept every night of my very young childhood. I remember the rattan barstools and the burnt-orange Formica countertops and the rust-colored medallions patterning the vinyl floors of the kitchen, where Mama prepared my Eggo waffle each morning, where she made the best strawberry milkshake I've ever had (she used a couple spoonfuls of strawberry jam, and it was what love tasted like). Christmas occurred in only one room in my memory: the formal living and dining area at the front of the house. The tree sat, lit with the rainbow of C9 color, in the bay window. There were bamboo sofas with silky floral cushions in shades of green and blue, with piping around the edges. Like outdoor furniture, but used indoors, they had the look of beachy eighties elegance. The brass peacock guarded the fireplace box, sooty from the rare and few fires Mississippi weather allowed. The formal dining table, where I once played with a brand-new electric typewriter, sat under the glow of the wood and glass china cabinet.

I cannot remember what was inside the china cabinet. I cannot remember if the floors were oak or pine in that room. I cannot remember the color of the hallway that kept us safe during the Glade tornado. Was it wallpapered? Was there paneling? I cannot remember exactly where my armoire sat in my bedroom, or if there was a closet inside my parents' bathroom. These things I cannot remember don't matter, not really, except that forgetting them feels like I am forgetting the eye color of someone whom I loved very much. I remember being loved and finding the first seedlings of my imagination and creativity in that house. I pass that house all the time, where baby swings now hang on the front porch. I wonder if there is still carpet in the den that those babies crawl on.

In 1992, when a local dentist made an offer on the old brick ranch, my parents built a new house next door, and we moved. It was southern traditional and very much in vogue for the 1990s in Mississippi. I slept there for the first time as a seven-year-old, and I am there two or three times a week still. I don't have to remember everything about this house because it is not in the past yet, but I find myself taking photographs of things I will miss someday. It might not always be ours, so I must own what I can from it: making a tiger costume with my mom at the breakfast table from a foam mattress topper, paint, and electrical tape; learning from my parents how to strain a mountain of berries to make one perfect pink jar of mayhaw jelly over the ceramic-top stove; the memory of Mama dropping a pickle jar on the Saltillo tile floor the week we moved in. The crash as it tumbled from the countertop sounded like the end of the world, a movie sound effect. She warned us to stay out of the kitchen until she had cleaned it all up to save our bare feet from a billion razor-sharp splinters of glass scattered like birdshot. We still found the glitter of it years afterward when the fridge was replaced. It comes to me now that when we remember the homes we grew up in, we are really remembering the ways we felt in them, the people who lived in them, and the ways they cared for us.

In 2015, my grandmother moved to assisted living after more than a decade of living alone since my grandfather's passing in 2001. In 1982, after selling my parents the original 1955 ranch (the one I was later born in), my grandparents had built another brick ranch on the back of the family property, over the pond and through the woods, in a thicket of pine trees, beside the two-acre garden they planted. Their house was the place my family had gathered every Sunday and holiday since. As my grandmother's spark and health became more fragile in 2014, I had the thought to photograph a few rooms of her house with my phone—her ordinary rooms, unchanging since my earliest memory, except for the addition of a walker. I looked at the images days later and felt haunted by them. Though she wasn't pictured in all of the photographs, she is there in every one. These photos became the impetus for writing this book, where by walking through each room and memory in the home Ben and I made together, we keep our life there alive forever. I hope it encourages you to walk through yours—rich with milestones and love and remembrance that outlasts trends and rugs and sofas—as well.

There is grief in letting a house go. This is what I wrote in March 2015, the day I realized my grandmother's home would soon be a new beginning for a stranger who wouldn't know that the piano in the living room, which we played on sick days spent at her house, was out of tune; a stranger who would eventually cook and eat and sleep there and paint the rooms different colors than the ones in the background of my memories:

Tonight, my heart is at her tidy little brick house just across the pond from my parents'. It's on her back porch, in the white rocking chairs where it always smells like four-o'clocks in bloom. It's in her bathroom with the red heat lamp that she would click on when I would spend the night as a child and take bubble baths with those flowery Avon potions. It's in the glass pitcher of fresh sweet tea, always in her refrigerator, with a crumpled, homemade aluminum foil lid. It's in her wallpapered and country blue dining room, and in the ring of bricks in the side yard where she would build campfires and roast marshmallows for me and my cousin Jim when we got to sleep over. It's in the red-and-white striped flannel blanket we would use to build forts in the living room with chair backs and rubber bands. It's in the Reader's Digest *condensed book hardbacks with the illustrated endsheets of ships and pirates that sit on the bookshelves in the living*

room. *It's in the secret passageway to the garage beside the fireplace, where they kept the firewood stacked for cold winter days. It's in her utility room with the wall of canned figs and tomatoes, empty Ball jars ready for summer's bounty. I know that those places aren't her, that a house does not make a home, but right now it feels like it.*

And months later, I wrote about moving her objects, her belongings, her life lived well, out of that house:

But the things I wanted pertained to my memories with Mammaw in her kitchen, where she taught me to make biscuits, her spicy rice, pie crust cookies. We would have late-night snacks when I slept over (mild cheddar cheese and Ritz crackers, with hot chocolate if that's what I wanted), and though she was the greatest cook in the world (fried chicken! macaroni and cheese! spaghetti and meatballs!), the only dish she never cared for enough to master was the grilled cheese sandwich (microwaved, yikes!). Those are the memories I return to the most of my time with her, and so today I brought home the things that made my heart cry out when I saw them: her Blue Willow and Currier and Ives china. The Christmas cookie jar she bought in 1997. The silverware we used at every Sunday lunch. One wooden chair, from the guest bedroom, sturdy and lovely. The red Dutch oven, the crevices and edges tarnished black from years of hot grease. The heavy cobalt blue canisters for flour, sugar, tea, and cornmeal. Inside the canisters I found her last ingredients, the old plastic scoops buried, ready for baking. The antique rotary phone on the wall by the door that I used to call my mama and say "Good night!" when they were away on overnight trips, leaving me with Mammaw and Pappaw to build campfires, chew sugarcane, put together puzzles. Thirty-one years of my life spent visiting my grandparents, and I pulled out of the driveway today with only a precious few things, an armload, that it felt like their souls are still attached to, even if a little dusty.

———

Ben and I believe so passionately in restoring old houses because it feels like we have a responsibility to keep the memory of people and places from being swept away. We recognize the humanity in a house: brokenness is not permanent, anything can be redeemed. Like people. I think that is why, back then walking through the emptied rooms of my mammaw's house, and still at the start of every demolition on *Home Town*, I find the raw vacancy of a house hard to look at. In the same way it must take surgeons time to get used

Your home does not look like a magazine
article, and it was never meant to. It is an
ever-evolving heirloom keeping step with the
humans who are the custodians of it.

to the sight of the blood of their work, the sight of a ramshackle vacancy is unsettling to me. Houses are built with intention and personal preference; they are human creations that reflect human longing: living rooms and babies' rooms, kitchens, porches—they are designed to keep us safe as we go about living and loving each other.

And so, this book is an exercise in documenting the home where Ben and I first became a family, and I invited other friends and family to do the same in their homes. We have taken staged photos of our home before, and those pictures portray a version of the truth—the most aesthetically pleasing truth. But people are not perfect, and neither are the homes that keep them. I asked these friends to photograph their rooms the way they actually live in them, unstaged, imperfect. I asked them to tell me what moments made their

houses feel like family members, and I hope it will encourage you to do the same. It is not only perfection that is worth documenting, but what is personal. Your home does not look like a magazine article, and it was never meant to. It is an ever-evolving heirloom keeping step with the humans who are the custodians of it. We are passing through, but our homes live on after us; they are passed down and re-envisioned. Document the experience of your evolving home as if it were your growing baby even when it is an imperfect composition of unsorted laundry and broken toys; capture its dimples and first steps, its smells and sounds. There is so much joy in opening up the baby book, isn't there? To compare the little black footprints to the shoes in the hall? Life is forever evolving, and our homes are proof. Look at how far we've come. ✿

Contributors

Keyanna Bowen

CITY, STATE: Salisbury, Maryland

PROFESSION: Photographer, designer, TV host

HOME DESIGNED BY: Keyanna Bowen

HOME PHOTOGRAPHED BY: Keyanna Bowen

INSTAGRAM: @eastandlane

Cat Bude

CITY, STATE: Normandy, France

PROFESSION: Photographer, writer, business owner, and founder of Rabbit Hill Lifestyle: online shop, markets and cooking workshops, and culinary tours

HOME DESIGNED BY: Unknown; built in 1640

HOME PHOTOGRAPHED BY: Cat Bude

INSTAGRAM: @cat_in_france

Caroline Burks

CITY, STATE: Laurel, Mississippi

PROFESSION: Owner of Guild and Gentry

HOME DESIGNED BY: Erin Napier, Blake Erskin, Amanda Connolly

HOME PHOTOGRAPHED BY: Brooke Davis-Jefcoat

INSTAGRAM: @guildandgentry

Linda Carson

CITY, STATE: Laurel, Mississippi

PROFESSION: doTERRA Wellness Advocate

HOME DESIGNED BY: Erin Napier, Blake Erskin, Amanda Connolly

HOME PHOTOGRAPHED BY: Brooke Davis-Jefcoat

Sandra M. Cavallo

CITY, STATE: Falmouth, Massachusetts

PROFESSION: Interior designer

HOME DESIGNED BY: Sandra M. Cavallo

HOME PHOTOGRAPHED BY: Sandra M. Cavallo

INSTAGRAM: @oldsilvershed

Cassidy Compton

CITY, STATE: Gadsden, Alabama

PROFESSION: Photographer

HOME DESIGNED BY: Cassidy Compton

HOME PHOTOGRAPHED BY: Cassidy Compton

INSTAGRAM: @nightensong

Louise Coster

CITY, STATE: Hingham, Norfolk, UK

PROFESSION: Antiques and reclamation dealer with her husband, Sam

HOME DESIGNED BY: Louise and Sam Coster

HOME PHOTOGRAPHED BY: Louise Coster

INSTAGRAM: @reclamationandroses

Anthony D'Argenzio

CITY, STATE: Hudson, New York

PROFESSION: Designer, entrepreneur, real estate connoisseur, father

HOME DESIGNED BY: Zio and Sons

HOME PHOTOGRAPHED BY: Zio and Sons

INSTAGRAM: @zioandsons

Brooke Davis-Jefcoat

CITY, STATE: Laurel, Mississippi

PROFESSION: Communications manager and photographer at Laurel Mercantile Co.

HOME DESIGNED BY: Erin Napier, Amanda Connolly, Whitney Blanchard, Gavrielle Mckinney

HOME PHOTOGRAPHED BY: Brooke Davis-Jefcoat

INSTAGRAM: @brookedavisjefcoat

Jennifer Faith

CITY, STATE: Searcy, Arkansas

PROFESSION: Physician

HOME DESIGNED BY: Jennifer Faith

HOME PHOTOGRAPHED BY: Jennifer Faith

INSTAGRAM: @faithmd

Brian Patrick Flynn

CITY, STATE: Atlanta, Georgia, and Reykjavík, Iceland

PROFESSION: Interior designer

HOME DESIGNED BY: Brian Patrick Flynn

HOME PHOTOGRAPHED BY: Robert Peterson

INSTAGRAM: @bpatrickflynn

Tessa Foley

CITY, STATE: Mariemont, Ohio

PROFESSION: Interior designer

HOME DESIGNED BY: Tessa Foley

HOME PHOTOGRAPHED BY: Tessa Foley

INSTAGRAM: @nineandsixteen

Victoria Ford

CITY, STATE: Cary, North Carolina
PROFESSION: Strategist
HOME DESIGNED BY: Victoria Ford
HOME PHOTOGRAPHED BY: Victoria Ford
INSTAGRAM: @prepfordwife

Emily James

CITY, STATE: Laurel, Mississippi
PROFESSION: Teacher
HOME DESIGNED BY: Erin Napier, Blake Erskin, Amanda Connolly
HOME PHOTOGRAPHED BY: Brooke Davis-Jefcoat

Lauren Liess

CITY, STATE: Great Falls, Virginia
PROFESSION: Interior designer
HOME DESIGNED BY: Lauren Liess
HOME PHOTOGRAPHED BY: Lauren Liess
INSTAGRAM: @laurenliess

Jenny Marrs

CITY, STATE: Bentonville, Arkansas
PROFESSION: Designer
HOME DESIGNED BY: Jenny Marrs
HOME PHOTOGRAPHED BY: Jenny Marrs
INSTAGRAM: @jennymarrs

Leigh and Ben Muldrow

CITY, STATE: Milford, Delaware
PROFESSION: Leigh is a landscape architecture designer, Ben is the owner of Arnett Muldrow & Associates
HOME DESIGNED BY: Leigh and Ben Muldrow
HOME PHOTOGRAPHED BY: Leigh Muldrow
INSTAGRAM: @house_1924

Lauren and Jesse Napier

CITY, STATE: Laurel, Mississippi
PROFESSION: Owners of Napier Frames
HOME DESIGNED BY: Erin and Ben Napier
HOME PHOTOGRAPHED BY: Brooke Davis-Jefcoat
INSTAGRAM: @napierframeslaurel

Kara and Brett Phillips

CITY, STATE: Fort Worth, Texas
PROFESSION: Owners of Phillips House, a design-build firm
HOME DESIGNED BY: Phillips House
HOME PHOTOGRAPHED BY: Brett Phillips
INSTAGRAM: @phillipshouse_

Layla Quilichini-Rovira

CITY, STATE: Fairfax, Virginia
PROFESSION: Housewife
HOME DESIGNED BY: Layla Quilichini-Rovira
HOME PHOTOGRAPHED BY: Layla Quilichini-Rovira
INSTAGRAM: @casa_de_layla

Karen Rasberry

CITY, STATE: Laurel, Mississippi
PROFESSION: Realtor
HOME DESIGNED BY: Karen Rasberry
HOME PHOTOGRAPHED BY: Brooke Davis-Jefcoat

Mallorie Rasberry

CITY, STATE: Laurel, Mississippi
PROFESSION: Co-owner of Rasberry Financial Services, Laurel Mercantile Co., and Scotsman Co.
HOME DESIGNED BY: Mallorie Rasberry
HOME PHOTOGRAPHED BY: Brooke Davis-Jefcoat
INSTAGRAM: @malraz

Rena Register

CITY, STATE: Ellisville, Mississippi
PROFESSION: Missional mobilization coordinator for Jones County Baptist Association, owner of Rena's House & Pet Sitting Service, and founder and creator of Jones Bones Dog Treats
HOME DESIGNED BY: Erin Napier, Amanda Connelly, Blake Erskin, Whitney Blanchard
HOME PHOTOGRAPHED BY: Brooke Davis-Jefcoat
INSTAGRAM: @Jonesboneslaurel

Emily and Grant Saxton

CITY, STATE: Laurel, Mississippi
PROFESSION: Emily is a nurse, Grant is a pediatrician
HOME DESIGNED BY: Erin Napier, Amanda Connolly, Whitney Blanchard, Emily Saxton
HOME PHOTOGRAPHED BY: Brooke Davis-Jefcoat

Linda and Drew Scott

CITY, STATE: Los Angeles, California

PROFESSION: Hosts of *At Home* podcast; TV host, producer

HOME DESIGNED BY: Linda and Drew Scott, Breeze Giannasio (bird room), Victoria Tonelli (attic and basement)

HOME PHOTOGRAPHED BY: Linda Phan Scott

INSTAGRAM: @athome

Aly Smith

CITY, STATE: Laurel, Mississippi

PROFESSION: Controller, Laurel Mercantile Co.

HOME DESIGNED BY: Erin Napier, Blake Erskin, Amanda Connolly

HOME PHOTOGRAPHED BY: Brooke Davis-Jefcoat

Liz Strong

CITY, STATE: Los Angeles, California

PROFESSION: Stylist/owner of Liz Strong Style, owner of Rush House

HOME DESIGNED BY: Liz Strong

HOME PHOTOGRAPHED BY: Liz Strong

INSTAGRAM: @lizstrongstyle

Erica Swagler

CITY, STATE: Alton, Illinois

PROFESSION: Vintage dealer, part-time legal assistant, part-time flute teacher

HOME DESIGNED BY: Builder unknown, interior by Erica Swagler

HOME PHOTOGRAPHED BY: Erica Swagler

INSTAGRAM: @living_in_a_landmark

Lily and Adam Trest

CITY, STATE: Laurel, Mississippi

PROFESSION: Lily is an art gallery owner, Adam is an artist

HOME DESIGNED BY: Architect: Chris Rischer Sr. Interiors: Lily Trest

HOME PHOTOGRAPHED BY: Brooke Davis-Jefcoat

INSTAGRAM: @carongallerysouth @adamtrest

Pathakone (Patti) Wagner

CITY, STATE: Minneapolis, Minnesota

PROFESSION: Designer, blogger, real estate investor

HOME DESIGNED BY: Patti Wagner

HOME PHOTOGRAPHED BY: Patti Wagner

INSTAGRAM: @patticakewagner

Amanda Watters

CITY, STATE: Kansas City, Missouri

PROFESSION: Shopkeeper of Homesong Market, a sustainable home goods store in Kansas City, Missouri, and blogger of *Homesong*, a seasonal lifestyle blog

HOME DESIGNED BY: Amanda Watters, architectural renovation by Cicada Co.

HOME PHOTOGRAPHED BY: Amanda Watters

INSTAGRAM: @mamawatters

Jennifer and Mike Weber

CITY, STATE: Laurel, Mississippi

PROFESSION: Jennifer is a homemaker, Mike is a physician

HOME DESIGNED BY: Jennifer Weber

HOME PHOTOGRAPHED BY: Brooke Davis-Jefcoat

Shellie Whitfield

CITY, STATE: Wetumpka, Alabama

PROFESSION: Artist/executive director of the Chamber of Commerce

HOME DESIGNED BY: Shellie Whitfield, Erin Napier, Vanessa Price

HOME PHOTOGRAPHED BY: Shellie Whitfield

INSTAGRAM: @big_fish_art_studio

1

Front Porch

I HEARD the swish of a broom on the front porch before I saw the woman sweeping as we walked past the straw-hued craftsman I'd noticed since I was in junior high school. To my surprise, stooped over focused on her task there beside the front door, white with fifteen window lights, was Mrs. Mary Lynn. If the house were a food, it would be a yellow coconut cake with white icing. My mouth watered every time I passed it on a million long walks with Ben early in our marriage. I felt most unneighborly when I realized I'd never known that the occupant of my beloved favorite house was right under my nose, two pews ahead of us at the church. She was one of the spry, cotton-haired congregants usually in a pastel skirt suit, always with a warm greeting during the passing of the peace. I shouted out to her that I had loved that house my whole life but never knew who lived in it, and she invited us in for the first time. The porch was my first meeting with what would be my forever home, and it made a winning impression.

The architectural purpose of a porch is a lower-ceilinged point of entry, a transition from street to house that provides shade, though Ben and I found it to be more than that. It was the smile on the front of that house, a grin from front to French doors, curling around the corner into an enclave in the shadow of its deep eaves with rafter tails like arms reaching for an embrace. Americans largely stopped building houses with porches for a time because more cars required wider roads, and the cool efficiency of interior air-conditioning made the option of sitting on the porch seem like an honorable mention ribbon in the blazing hot summer. I feel sorry for houses without porches, though. If houses with porches are the huggers of architecture, the non-porched are those houses that offer a stiff handshake at first meeting.

When we bought the house in September 2011, we set about adding our own chapter to its eighty-six-year-long story. The first step in effectively changing the personality to something more akin to our old souls was to replace the mostly glass front door with an antique craftsman-style door we found at an architectural salvage place in Jackson. We spent days stripping layer after layer of paint from the old door: white, salmon, maroon, seafoam, until finally, after our hands were blistered from scraping, we got down to the bare fir. We stained it Early American and clear-coated

it and hung that old door with great care, but it never quite complied. It always stuck a little on one side when you tried to open it, but it was only seventy-five dollars so we pretended not to notice (and ultimately replaced it with a heavy solid-oak reproduction of a 1920s door in 2016). Step two in the transformation was the easiest: changing the "classic gray porch" floor paint to something more at home in a 1920s color story. After much trial and error during pollen season, we arrived at the perfect golden-olive color to disguise both Pine Belt pollen and muddy size 14 work boot tracks.

Our first purchases for the porch were shoddy, cheap Adirondack chairs and a five-foot glider swing that looked like teak from the street, but felt like the paper-weight wood they use to make those little glider airplanes. Each piece left something to be desired—namely, quality—but it was what we could afford at the time. Soon we acquired a frilly antique wooden table, about three feet by three feet with turned legs and rounded corners, and mismatched wooden dining chairs that made a fine spot to have a meal under the ceiling fan, and we put a floor lamp beside the table in the corner, because it made us feel Parisian to have dinner al fresco by lamplight.

As we saved our money to replace our pitiful first porch furnishings, which were quickly ravaged by humidity and mildew, the final piece

If houses with porches
are the huggers of architecture, the
non-porched are those houses
that offer a stiff handshake at
first meeting.

of the porch puzzle was a big, generous swing for napping and swaying, big enough to carry a giant man and a normal-sized girl side by side. Ben built the swing in his shop from hundred-year-old heart pine that will take decades for the sun and rain to finally batter down to splinters. It reminds me of a finely handcrafted boat, low to the floor, suspended from four hardy ropes, topped with two enormous cushions that make up the size of a twin bed mattress. With two topiaries in jugs flanking the front door and real teak dining furniture and Adirondacks, our porch has reached its current (and we hope lasting) design iteration. This porch is the setting for the story of our family and how it grew and how we learned about hospitality.

The porch was a soft landing the morning of my infant nephew's adoption hearing. The weeks leading up to that day were rife with heartache and anxiety, my mother racked with sobs on the kitchen floor when she got the call that the birth father was backpedaling on the adoption after this baby boy had been in my brother's and his wife's arms for six months, since the day he was born. The cold marble courtroom felt grim, but my brother came ready to fight for his son under those fluorescent lights, their attorney at his side, a steady hand and trusted friend of our family.

Ten fast minutes into the proceedings, before our seats had even warmed, the judge asked the birth father, "Do you contest the adoption of the child?"

He said, "No, I'll sign the waiver."

Without explanation, he gave up his rights to my nephew.

The judge declared the baby ours. We were prepared for battle, not a white flag, and so a last-minute celebration gathered around the dinner table on our front porch, just a few steps from the courthouse. April in Mississippi is about the best time you'll get for an honest-to-God porch party, and by 11 a.m., we were licking fried chicken grease from our fingers and toasting with cheap champagne, the best we could find under the circumstances, in paper Dixie cups. My brother was stunned and quiet, laying down the weapons in his heart, as his wife bounced that fat, drooling baby boy on her knee. My nephew was born all over again that day on my porch, six months after taking his first breath.

Four years later, another new life joined our family when our daughter Helen was born. When she was six months old, our front porch became her first playground. Her nanny, Mimi, would lay quilts on the floor and set up a bouncer in front of our security camera so Ben and I could watch Helen from our phones on set as she bounced 178 times in a row, stopping only to examine a fire truck racing down our street, or to babble

at the standard poodle and his owner who walk the block every morning at 10 a.m. No matter where we were during the workday, maybe in the grime of a moldy kitchen or learning the fine art of attic bat extraction, with our phones and a doorbell camera we could teleport to Helen on that porch with her Mimi, eating her very first doughnut hole on the porch swing her daddy had built, cooing to Dolly Parton playing quietly in the background. Now, at age four, she sends us off every morning by standing atop the armrests of the porch swing, leaning out as she hangs from its ropes, shouting to us in her nightgown and house shoes. She is on a boat departing the seashore, and the day is an adventure stretched in front of her as we pull out of the driveway for work and leave her in Mimi's care: "Bye, Mama and Daddy! I love you! The coast is clear! You're a good mama and daddy! Be careful! See you later! See you at lunch! Make good choices!"

There is a pear tree in the yard of our house that Mrs. Mary Lynn's husband planted twenty years ago. The spring when my best friend, Mallorie, was pregnant, she saw a pear tree at my grandmother's house that was bursting with white blooms; she said, "When those pears are ripe, the baby will be here," her hand resting on her growing belly. In August, dressed in overalls and a kerchief tied around my hair, I climbed a nine-foot ladder beside our pear tree, channeling my grandmother, the goddess of canning and "putting up," who feared only one thing in this life: an empty deep freeze. I sweated and swayed on that ladder, plucking my harvest from the tree's limbs and dropping them into four five-gallon buckets on the grass. I was determined to pick it clean, to see the limbs sprung back up into the sky from my kitchen sink, to know I had done good work and picked my own fruit and canned it, too.

It turns out it takes just five gallons of pears to make exactly two pear cakes with caramel icing and to learn your limit on a first-time canning experience (complete with Red Hots in some of the jars for Christmas and Instagram). I sat three buckets of pears on my porch with a note scrawled on the back of a cardboard box lid: FREE TO A GOOD HOME!

I left one cake on the kitchen counter at Mallorie and my cousin Jim's house the morning after Lucy was born, a celebration of their own new tiny harvest. I took the other cake to Mrs. Mary Lynn at her new condo; her old porch had welcomed so much new life in the short history of my and Ben's marriage and taught me important lessons in being neighborly. If the back porch is where we can let our hair down in solitude, the front porch is our Sunday best, a hug after the service, a potluck dinner of fried chicken and champagne. ✿

MALLORIE RASBERRY Our porch is ground zero on Halloween night. Halloween in Laurel is so magical—our entire street shuts down and there are thousands of kids who trick-or-treat all evening. Our family and friends come over, help give out candy, and have the best time. It's definitely one of my most favorite traditions that come with living on this street.

11

MALLORIE RASBERRY

LAYLA QUILICHINI-ROVIRA

LINDA CARSON   When I turned the corner of our little street for the first time, I had to park on the side of the road just to take in the beautiful scene before me! I knew immediately this house was the one. The azaleas were in full bloom on this tree-lined avenue with vintage lampposts, and I just knew this had to be the most beautiful street in Laurel. When I finally tore myself away from the view, I continued to drive under the lush, overhanging boughs of the ancient oaks and came upon a FOR SALE sign. I knew this house was the one, because it had that sign out front and because when we entered the living room, it was awash with the most ethereal light coming in through the glass panes of the original sash windows!

SANDRA M. CAVALLO The original home on the property my husband and I purchased was an old Folk Victorian from 1905; our dream was to build onto the home and create a great space for our family. Unfortunately, the home had been abandoned and uncared for just too long, so we were not able to safely work with it, but we used the disappointment as an opportunity. We carefully began to dismantle it piece by piece and saved every piece we could, and began to build from there. To pay homage to the original cottage, in my family room we re-created the identical entryway of the original home. We used the same pitch in the roof, added the same dormer, and it added a special nod to the past. We were able to save the beach rock fireplace in the library, some of the original transom windows. So although the original home we purchased no longer stands, we honored our favorite parts in the home that stands today.

CASSIDY COMPTON I will never forget the first time I sat out here with one of my children. We were so amazed at our new porch, that it was ours to enjoy, and we did. Birds in our trees were singing, our new neighbors were walking past on the sidewalk, and we felt the breeze. We just sat there together really enjoying it, and I remember that happy feeling perfectly. Rain or shine, it's a place where we spend so much time all year long.

CASSIDY COMPTON When I walked inside, I felt like I was walking into the past. I thought that I'd never seen an old home restored so thoughtfully to its origin, architecturally speaking. Or maybe it was because no big architectural changes had ever been made. The original woodwork was so beautiful with a deep, rich stain and it sang. The wavy lead-glass windows (which work!) turn our outdoor views into paintings. There were two big porches, and a yard that felt like a secret garden. We pictured so many happy memories and knew it was built to withstand our boys, who love skateboarding down the long, wide halls. With all that heavy wainscoting they couldn't hurt this house. It was a gem of a historic home. I first told my husband while viewing it, "There isn't much I want to change here," and that's a rare thing for him to hear me say. I just wanted to repaint, make it better in a few shabby corners, and make it ours. When we learned there were only two families to ever live here, and that both of their last names started with a C too, it felt right. This house was the perfect size for my husband and me and our four boys, whose shared rooms are connected. I say all of the time, this house is just right, and it has loved us back.

———

Home Town Takeover, Season 1

THE WHITFIELD HOUSE

Helping renovate the *Big Fish* house in Wetumpka, Alabama,
on *Home Town Takeover* was a highlight of my career
because it's my favorite movie of all time. It was important to me
that we not take away what makes the home iconic on film:
it is like a representation of heaven and peace, a goal achieved for
the character Edward Bloom, shiny and pure white. The
exterior was kept mostly the same for visitors with the exception
of yellow on the front door, a nod to Shellie, the artist who now
lives inside and fears no bold paint color in her work.

—*ERIN*

SHELLIE WHITFIELD The rockers on my front porch are from the
Big Fish movie and Jessica Lange rocked in them.

2

Entry

THE ENTRY sets the agenda of a home: it tells visitors what they can expect as they proceed farther in. In my home, it is a hill of size 14 boots piled near the shoe cabinet, not inside it, a thousand various pink backpacks stuffed with pocket change, fast-food toys, and ballet shoes that hang from hooks under the powdered noses of my grandmothers' pearl-earringed portraits. The guts of the day's delivery packages are stacked on the table that was intended to hold a neat tray of mail, proof of our finer nature, but here we are. We are more-is-more people who meant to be more elegant, and our foyer tells on us. The first time we walked through the front door of our house with Mrs. Mary Lynn, there was a polished antique walnut secretary holding three gilded-framed memories of her now-grown grandchildren, and a thriving, positively thrilled houseplant sitting atop a tiny marble table made specifically for that purpose. The pale-sage-green walls displayed exactly two pieces of art, both florals, and confirmed what I

The entry sets the agenda of a home: it tells visitors what they can expect as they proceed farther in.

already suspected about Mrs. Mary Lynn: she is polished, reliable, fast-food-less.

The great transformation of our home's interior began in that room, while the others remained mostly empty save for a few thrift store finds to get us through until the real things came along. We painted the walls the color of World War II fatigues and left the cream color on the picture rail and trim. My mother's back door entry displays a framed smattering of my ancestors' unhappy nineteenth-century faces and sack clothes alongside the flirty 1940s smiles and kitten heels of my grandmother curled into my handsome grandfather's arms, and I always wondered how those people could possibly be related. When I moved into my first home, I rummaged through Ben's and my parents' hope chests and sticky photo albums and found pictures that reminded me of fashion magazines, but of our people. Our very old people when they were very young, doing what young people do. Swimming in icy spring-fed ponds, swinging from the old magnolia tree, posing in velvet skirt suits with red coon dogs that died in 1952. My maternal grandmother's heart-shaped face smiles demurely beside the photo of my mama and her regionally famous legs in cutoff denim. I framed twenty of them in dollar-store wood frames and arranged them tightly, smothering

the wall around an old church pew: *This we do in remembrance of you.* I stole my mother's hammered copper umbrella stand, which she still asks when I will return knowing full well I never will, and filled it with hand-carved walking sticks atop which Ben's cowboy hats sit like hungry, skinny men on the range.

The French doors in the foyer open to the breakfast table on the front porch and allow a little river of hose water inside every time we wash the porch, no matter how firmly we closed them. To make another barrier against the elements, Ben built the custom screen doors early in his woodworking hobby, and it satisfied my wish to hear them sing their creak-slam songs as we came and went. Coming and going. To work, to faraway places, and home again. In my mind's eye I can still see the ramshackle luggage we bought for a two-week adventure to California before we could afford better, waiting in the entry to be loaded into our truck. That scene evolved to feature matching leather and waxed canvas sets that made us proud coming off the carousel at JFK in New York.

When Helen was born in 2018, we added tiny coats and crocheted hats that looked like strawberries or unicorns to the coatrack on the family history wall. Soon the size 1 baby moccasins by the door grew to size 5 Velcro sneakers

and she toddled over to kiss us good-bye each morning on our way out the door. Ben would kneel on the Persian and sisal rugs layered on the floor, then crouch down farther still to hold her miniature body. She didn't know or care that we were leaving then, but it crushed us, the leaving, with her nanny, Mimi, ready to whisk her away to read and paint and play naked in the backyard until we dragged in from a construction site at 5 p.m., Ben's muddy boots by the door punctuating the end of the day.

Coming home is like dessert now. There is such sweetness at the end of hard days and it crushes us all over again. We hear the delighted shriek of a nearly-four-year-old pounding toward us: "Mama! Daddy! Are you back for real?" And there she is, wrapping our knees in urgent hugs, dressed in a purple ballet leotard and light-up rabbit ears, glossy black tap shoes on her feet, my grandmother's heart-shaped face and my mother's legs coming into focus. One day she will stack her own mismatched luggage by this door for her daddy to load into the car, headed to a university somewhere.

But for today, she is little, and we are back for real. ✸

ADAM TREST I'll never forget walking through this house for the first time. The first room you walk into is the atrium, and there were no plants. The fountain had been drained; the room was just completely empty. The living room had a GIANT television covering the beautiful fireplace, the studio was being used as storage . . . but through all of that, after seeing the whole house, I remember looking at Lily and saying, "This is it." There are houses, and then there is architecture, and this house is the latter. Every inch of this house was designed and thought over—some spaces we didn't even realize how designed they were until months after we moved in.

———

Home Town, Season 2

THE SMITH HOUSE

There is not another house in Laurel in the architectural style
of Aly and Jordan's home, with its Italianate-inspired
arches and tiled front porch. The challenge was taking their
North Mississippi and Delta-infused background and making it sing
in harmony with this more formal European architecture. Finding
ways to make the interior feel casually collected
but moody enough to carry the gravitas was fun. In particular,
collecting hand-knotted Turkish rugs and stitching them together to
construct the stair runner was a favorite project for me.

—ERIN

CASSIDY COMPTON The foyer ceiling goes all the way up to the second floor above the stairs, and it is as big as our other main rooms. Every Christmas we take advantage of the space with a huge fifteen-foot tree that we bought secondhand. It takes us days to work out the sections of lights that stopped working and then to put our ornaments all the way to the top. It's a challenge that we as a family work together to accomplish, even down to the ornaments we make or find for each other, and we end up with something completely enchanting and special to us.

CAT BUDE I knew the house was special from the first moment of our initial visit. The way it sat just slightly up a hill, in a stark sort of way. It was like it was saying, "Here I am!" When we first walked through, I was stunned by the tiles and then the staircase that divides the center of the house—its uneven treads, twisted banister, and wonky angles, as if through the years it stretched and bent as the house settled into its spot on the ground. I will never again be able to live in a house with average or low ceilings, or one without massive beams or ancient doors. And every single imperfection made it feel even more like home.

EMILY JAMES I knew this house was the one when I saw the hardwood floors, natural lighting, cased openings, and location.

———————

Home Town, Season 3
THE SAXTON HOUSE

I admired the Saxton home on walks for years, when the
Ford family lived there and then later when other families passed through
for a time. It had an English town-and-country elegance, shaded by the
oaks in the yard; it was always a bit mysterious. The hallway and its
many additions presented a problem because of ceiling height differences
in each new section added over the decades. Building arches at every
juncture solved the problem and elevated the European style even more.
Adding a Dutch door was a must for me, knowing they saw a future with
dogs and babies and cookouts in that courtyard. It's such a charming
outdoor space—like a Nancy Meyers movie.

—ERIN

EMILY SAXTON The mudroom is the perfect "plop spot," as my husband says. We kick our shoes off, take our hats and coats and hang them here, and this is the main entry into our home. I love that access to our laundry room is right here as well. This room feels like a reminder for us to take a load off and be home. A favorite piece in this room is the large quilt we keep on the shelf to grab for picnics at the park with our little family.

ERICA SWAGLER Walking through the front door and into the parlor to the left, I have a distinct memory of goose bumps and a warm feeling washing over me. There is a feeling and presence in this house—a good presence that drew me and my husband in, despite all the work and maintenance that we knew would be involved with owning such an old home.

JENNIFER FAITH   The entry has a favorite gallery wall of antique oil portraits that I love to see. It also has old rugs and an old piece of furniture that I store lots of bakeware in. My dogs love to run down the stairs and mess the rugs up, so I have to constantly fix them, but secretly I love it!

JENNIFER WEBER I love coming in the front door and seeing the wonderful watercolor Adam Trest did years ago of our home.

IN THE FAMILY

———

My parents' house

This is the house where I grew up, where Mama dropped
the pickle jar, where Helen took her first steps, and where I brought
home a boy named Ben to meet my parents, who fell in love
with him just as hard as I did. All my life's most pivotal memories
before I had a family of my own happened in these rooms,
and I feel there will always be beauty in the high-quality materials
my parents chose when building the house in 1992. That oak
kitchen and Saltillo tile will never go out of style!

—*ERIN*

ALY SMITH Walking into the foyer for our reveal on *Home Town* is maybe my favorite memory in this room. The relief of not having red monkey wallpaper and green carpet was pretty intense.... Our foyer just kind of has a way of feeling like a warm hug. Natural light from the windows, the vintage runner on the staircase, pieces of furniture from both of my grandmothers, artwork from the Laurel Mercantile that I picked and framed . . .

LEIGH MULDROW I'm not sure that we have specific memories in the mudroom, but it might be the most important room in the house! The room had been paneled in the 1950s and initially we thought we could keep it natural, but there was significant water damage and finding boards cut with the same pattern proved impossible, so we slept on it and decided to paint it. It's one of my favorite rooms in the house because it really tells the story of everything we do—all our different shoes and coats and activity bags—just a catchall for family life. We don't fuss over how tidy it is (or isn't) because it really does the job of keeping the daily clutter right there: its job is to be messy so the rest of the house stays under control. We intentionally left the hooks and bench open and the shoe bins without baskets—having eighteen years of parenting under our belts has taught us that the easier you make it, the more likely it is the kids will use it, and this is absolutely true in this space. It's more important to us to be able to find both shoes quickly than to run around frantically because having a basket just encouraged them to take their shoes off by the couch instead.

LIZ STRONG The Austrian bell jar lantern is an antique and was given to us by a friend from their childhood home overseas. The large photograph of the Indian soldier was taken by a photographer friend and given to us as a wedding gift. The other pieces of art were flea market finds. The vintage wash pail, folding egg crate, and Oushak rug are from my favorite vendor at the local flea market. The chair is a family heirloom we re-covered. The glass soldier is a collectible from Nassau that was a gift. I chose the wallpaper for its vintage appeal. It is graphic yet it felt like it belonged in this house— it is from Quadrille. The front door and flush-mount fixture are original to the home.

PATTI WAGNER The foyer is the one room that stays the tidiest for some reason. I love how the sunlight makes this room glow in the morning when I walk downstairs. I also enjoy getting the mail from the little mailbox here. My favorite is that our girls often will leave us notes in the mailbox and ask us, "Did you check the mail today?"

———

Home Town, Season 5

THE NAPIER HOUSE

The great advantage of designing a home for my brother-
and sister-in-law is that we spent years in advance daydreaming with
them of their someday home. All the wonderful weirdness about
their love for the 1970s mashed up with 1990s style meeting in a historic
little house gave us so many wonderful tools to make this layered
cottage for them. I used sentimental passed-down furniture, pieces Jesse
built for Lauren when he worked in Ben's woodshop, thrifted
art, saturated color, and modern fixtures to tell the whole story of who
they are: young with old souls, never fussy, a bit eccentric.

—*ERIN*

VICTORIA FORD
We customized this home, and each step along the way of us customizing it, we infused it with ourselves and our memories.

LOUISE COSTER Many of the items and building materials we use are reclaimed, so they all have a story to tell. The nicest thing is making new memories with them, together with our family and friends.

3

Living Room

I SOMETIMES think of people of the past and their formal living rooms and wonder what sort of living they did there. Were their conversations with friends as formal as their thin jacquard sofas with wooden arms? As proper as the cut crystal candy dishes filled with mints? Were those rooms only an indication of status, not meant to be lived in? I know from the photos of my grandparents in my entryway that these people were fun, they danced and laughed and made mischief same as us, told improper jokes and wore their skirts a little shorter than their mothers would have liked. Surely they had a room for informal visits with friends and family. If there is a living room where no one ever snuggled into the furniture with a mug of hot tea, where children have never made tents and floor pallets (or puppy beds, as Helen calls them) on a stormy day, where a piecemealed quilt has never been tossed over the sofa arm for when fall brings its first chill to the house, where books are not huddled together on every available surface, I'm

We had seven years in this house without children, but my memories of it without Helen or Mae in it are few.

unsure of how to use it. A living room ought to be where we do our living, unselfconsciously. In pants with elastic waistbands.

The first time we saw our house's living room, it was an untouched grand parlor with sheer white curtains and an elegant mirror above the fireplace. The family before us used a small room off the foyer as a little den for their party of two, and it suited them. They were not people with a need for sprawling comfort, and it was not yet the home of a giant and his overly sentimental wife given to collecting. The room was the color of a lemon meringue pie, all buttoned-up formality and polished heart pine floors that had not seen a toddler spill grape juice in many years. We were childless then, but I knew what that room would become for us: the glowing hearth of our home and future family life. Now, ten years on, it is the room I fantasize about returning to while nervously cruising at forty thousand feet on our way to the hustle of a few New York City media days, or at 3 p.m. in the August sun on a filthy construction site as sweat rolls down my spine.

In the fall of 2011, a few days after we closed on the house, we spent one late night with a handful of friends painting the rooms of our new home. Three boxes of Papa Johns pizza and the Avett Brothers on the radio were our modest offerings of thanks. We rolled and brushed, cutting in around the trim at 1 a.m. with bleary eyes before calling it a night. My mother spent a day not long after that cutting and hemming a dozen canvas drop cloths that would make fine impersonators of the expensive linen curtain panels I'd wanted but our artist and student minister budgets wouldn't allow. We blitzed the Mississippi flea market circuit on the hunt for a factory cart that would be our coffee table, and eventually settled on a manufactured impostor that would pass for the real thing in a photo. A heavy old nineteenth-century chopping block that we found in Jackson was worn down in waves from the butcher's knife and it looked like an end table to me, so we brought it in next to our canvas-slipcovered sofa. You could see it had a sordid past, so I sprayed a little Lysol on it and lifted it up in my prayers that night. We covered the north wall of the room in bookcases and filled the shelves quickly by bringing home any secondhand-store hardcovers that sounded remotely interesting. The new additions kept company with our old books and another massive collection of black-and-white family photos, this time of Ben's family—weaving the threads of ancestry through our house. Our favorite images are those we called "Wayne Riding on Things": Ben's daddy on horses, bicycles, tractors, cars, trucks.

I turned the stuffy sconces upside down, and replaced the glass shades that looked like lilies with new linen ones. I brought over the oil portrait of a World War II sailor that was living at our old loft, and perched a brass picture light above it that has never since been turned off. Three other lamps all burn dimly with 40-watt bulbs. We have an overhead light in that room, but it's never been turned on. I find the dimness cozy, like dinner by candlelight.

In the years that followed, our two sofas and one armchair were witness to late-night chats with friends who had come to visit from near and far. When Mallorie was unknowingly pregnant with Lucy in 2012 and feeling the heavy tiredness of the first trimester, she fell asleep with her head in Jim's lap on our sofa two nights in a row while we were watching movies. Both times, as the credits rolled, we turned out the lights and pulled a quilt over her so she could sleep through the night. One December weekend, our friend Suss came to town with her sister and brother-in-law, Morgane and Chris Stapleton. That weekend we set Suss up on a blind date with a guy named Ben Cole, and it turned into a marriage a few months later. The night they met, we were all headed to the art museum gala in our finest gowns and tuxedos and overcoats, and took photographs by the firebrick and Saltillo

tile hearth as if we were going to prom, but without the corsages and curfews. Our friends Rachel and Chris Sullivan spent one week with us in July, and every night after the babies were in bed we set up their three monitors on the coffee table and talked until midnight about music and acting and building. The quiet shush of the baby sound machines assured us they weren't stirring, and if one cried out in their sleep, we all reached for the monitors to see whose number was up.

We had seven years in this house without children, but my memories of it without Helen or Mae in it are few. It was a beautiful living room before them. It became a real, loved room after, like the Velveteen Rabbit. The freezing cold January day we brought Helen home from the hospital, we walked inside with hushed reverence. That day, for the first time, we were someone's mama and daddy, and she crossed the threshold in our arms. I've imagined thousands of times in her life to come when she will walk through that door, seeking solace in the living room in different circumstances: in Halloween costumes, after suffering heartbreaks, on the way to her wedding. That first day, I held her and explained as Ben filmed it: "This is your house. This is our living room. This is your swing in the window. This will be your rocking horse when you're bigger. This is where we get warm by the fire. This

is home." For Valentine's Day, a month later, Ben surprised me with a handcrafted coffee table: four feet by four feet, with heart pine tongue-and-groove on top framed by oak, a dado-jointed rack below to store toy baskets, and hand-turned spooled legs made from oak that mimicked her crib. That coffee table taught Helen how to walk after steadying her wobbly little body for months; then it became her easel and painting studio, where we would leave out a palette of watercolors and a mug of water and brushes beside her sketch pad for quick access whenever creativity struck. It is the puzzle table, the toddler-height break-fast, lunch, and dinner table. It is the fulcrum of her routines.

From Thanksgiving to New Year's Day, our living room transforms. Each year we spend a weekend turning the airy cream and blue room into a richly festive New England–inspired den with evergreen boughs draped across the bookcases, red shades on the sconces, and a nine-foot Fraser fir where the baby swing once sat, shimmering with old-world glass fig-urines and corny, sentimental ornaments from our life's story together that are priceless to us, a red-striped roll of upholstery webbing weav-ing around its branches, behind and through the lights. Wool plaid stockings hang from the mantel, a Christmas movie always on rotation or Elvis singing Christmas songs ever present on the speakers throughout the house. When I'm old I'll still remember Christmas mornings with our baby when she could walk for the first time, finding the toy kitchen Ben built for her the night before, the rolling mountains of ripped and wadded gift wrap, knee-deep scraps of a happy Christmas morning.

One year, a week before Christmas, the Mississippi weather turned unusually sinister. A tornado came barreling toward downtown Laurel as we were just pulling a roasted rose-mary chicken out of the oven to eat dinner with our brother and sister-in-law, Jesse and Lauren. The tornado siren a block from our house began its wailing. We scooped up Helen and all ran to fold ourselves into the half bath under the stairs together. Just as we closed the door, the lights went out and we heard the angry crash of glass and wood, the awful bellowing of wind around the rafters. The house came alive in a way I'd never felt, bearing down, groaning against the wind. For the first time in my life I truly under-stood the word *shelter*. I cried out and cradled Helen so close I could smell the applesauce on her breath as she screamed, "The thunder is get-ting us!"

> We left that one mullion unpainted
> on the inside, a deep red scar on the white window
> above the couch that we could always see to
> remember that storm.

When the world fell quiet again, the power was gone, and we rushed around the house looking for the damage and found it in the living room: debris from the storm had smashed our front windows. Amid the tree limbs, broken glass and ornaments glittered on the Persian rug with one of Helen's tiny pink hair bows in the beam of our flashlight. We spent the night at my parents' after helping neighbors cut limbs out of their driveways and off the roads, assessing the damage in the pitch-dark city by the glow of our headlights, dressed in pajamas and boots. A few days later, Ben came home from the woodshop and unscrewed the plywood we'd hurriedly applied to the windows in the hours after the storm. He had carefully milled a piece of mahogany to exactly replicate the original 1925 mullions to replace one that was broken in the storm. He glazed around the new piece of glass, careful to keep the glazing compound off the mahogany. We left that one mullion unpainted on the inside, a deep red scar on the white window above the couch that we could always see to remember that storm and the way our house had cradled us like a mother, keeping us safe.

Three and a half years after Helen was born, we came home to the quiet again with Mae in our arms, only this time our living room was cluttered with the colorful evidence of childhood. Helen was on the way with her Mimi after swimming that afternoon. We placed Mae in the same swing that had showed Helen the frozen outside world through the windows that winter, but this time the apple tree was a deep spring green. Helen came bursting through the door, in tears with excitement and happiness: her best friend was finally born, and she asked if she could please hold her. We sat her in the blue-striped chair by the hearth and placed her baby sister in her arms. Helen cooed and giggled and stared at Mae, lovestruck. Mae opened her newborn eyes and mouth into a grin, even though newborns cannot grin, say the books. But that day she did. My heart exploded and I felt salty tears rising up from a lump in my throat. I could see our future coming toward us, moving at warp speed, with these two magical girls teaching us as we go. For all the living we had done in this room in ten years, none of it made me feel so alive as this. ❀

ADAM TREST The living room is full of books. It's full of the children's books of my childhood that have inspired me as an illustrator. It has embarrassing high school yearbooks, and special books that were gifted from friends. This room has some of my favorite pieces of art. Pieces we bought when we should have been saving money, pieces we bought at estate sales for five dollars only to find out they were worth MUCH more.

My favorite piece in there is the really strange blue-and-green tapestry wingback chair. The seat is octagonal, and the legs are in the front, back, left, and right instead of on the corners. The back is very narrow, but taller than normal. Needless to say, I love every part of it. It's one of the first pieces of furniture that I ever purchased—I found it in a consignment shop in Stuart, Florida, one summer during college, and I've drug it around to everywhere I've lived since. It's safe to say that almost everything in that room has a story.

AMANDA WATTERS When walking through this room the first time we immediately knew it needed warming up, and that natural materials, plus a wood-burning stove, something we've always wanted, could do just that. I love the charm of quaint cottages found throughout the English countryside, and that feeling is what inspired my design choices for this space, hence the large stone hearth, wide pine floorboards, and hand-hewn beams making a statement that says, "Cozy up!" It has been completely transformed and is by far the most relaxing room in the house, perfect for watching movies and lounging by the fire. The branches were foraged in our yard, and the antique chair found at a thrift shop.

ANTHONY D'ARGENZIO The moment I uncovered original wallpaper during the renovation—it's from the 1900s—I loved it so much that I was inspired to create a wallpaper line and even designed one of the styles to honor the aesthetic.

BRIAN PATRICK FLYNN One of my best friends, Robert, a professional photographer, took that image above the sofa of the Icelandic horse when we were exploring the country in March of 2016. That photo inspired the design, palette, and mood of the entire house. It sparks a sense of adventure and mystery and also a quiet calm, and that sums up the entire vibe of Iceland.

BROOKE DAVIS-JEFCOAT   The family room, while large and in charge in our house, still brings on a sense of warmth that I always knew it could have. Little places for the kids to leave their toys about and sit in the throne chair, as we call it, and read their favorite books— these are a few of our favorite things. In the winter we cozy up with lots of blankets and sit by the crackling fire, and in the summer we let the cool breeze of the air conditioning fill the room as we play chase from one end to the other. The old chair in the corner has been the landing place for so many cuddles when our big boy has bumps or bruises, and the toy box holds memories from a life long gone but always, always in our hearts. Sometimes when I'm picking up in the late afternoon and the sun hits it just so, I remember what that wood used to be and I smile and feel so thankful for these walls that it's now within.

CAROLINE BURKS   Our living room is part jungle gym, and every day when Cory gets home, Livi demands to "swing"—he picks her up, swings her back and forth a few times, and tosses her into the pillows on the couch. She'll do it as long as he'll let her, giggling the whole time. That's the best sound in the world.

JENNIFER WEBER (OPPOSITE)
It brings me great joy to have a second generation enjoying the train table in our den. I love to hear children making the sounds of trains running up and down the tracks.

EMILY JAMES (ABOVE AND RIGHT)
My favorite memory in the living room is gathering as a family to watch movies and sporting events, cuddling with my kids on the sofa; it's the room I always feel most comfortable in.

JENNIFER FAITH The living room is where I pile up on the couch with our two dogs and read a book or take naps. I enjoy catching up on shows with my family in the evenings.

KEYANNA BOWEN   We live on the Eastern Shore of Maryland, so during the winter months we don't get much snow. But our first winter in our rental, Mother Nature graced us with a record-breaking storm. We lit the fire, curled up on the sofa, and watched the snow fall from the large windows in our living room. It was magical.

76

KAREN RASBERRY My favorite memory in the living room is every Christmas since 1992. My favorite objects are a framed navigational map of the Normandy beaches that my daddy brought home after D-Day and a portrait of my granddaughter Helen, painted by the world-famous art forger Mark Landis. We'll never get rid of the rust-colored oversized chair and ottoman that have been putting folks to sleep for decades.

LAUREN LIESS My favorite memory from the living room is hanging out by the fire with the family talking, listening to music, reading out loud.

LAUREN NAPIER Jesse and I love the original hardwood floors, the square footage, and the three-bedroom and two-bathroom layout. We also enjoy the proximity to downtown Laurel and our quiet neighborhood.

LAYLA QUILICHINI-ROVIRA Each room in our town house flows easily into another. I love how our main living area is used on the daily. Our home is very well loved and that is my favorite memory. Knowing that every little area in our home serves a purpose and it is truly loved.

LINDA CARSON Our coffee table, made of salvaged walls and newel posts from an old Pennsylvania farmhouse, has weathered many moves, both in the States and across Europe.

MALLORIE RASBERRY   I love *Home Town* nights! The Napiers and friends always come over, we do pizza on the porch, toss the girls in the bath . . . then head into the family room, where we crowd around the TV and watch each episode together for the first time. We tell stories and reminisce about each episode. It's a comfortable space to lounge and gather. It's not lost on us— the surrealness of this season of life we are living and celebrating in this room . . . the same room where the Gilchrist family [one of Laurel's original timber families] used to host and dream up grand ideas for Laurel so many years ago. We hope they would be proud.

MALLORIE RASBERRY

RENA REGISTER One of my favorite things is the old library ladder that I salvaged from a house in North Laurel. It was discarded in a trash pile. My grandmother's Bible can also be found on my side table. I touch it almost daily. It has her name engraved in the lower corner. When I was young, the living room had a quilting rack that occupied nearly the whole room. My granny was a master at quilting. I remember sitting in that living room and asking her to tell me stories. Even as a young child I loved looking through her old black-and-white pictures that were kept in an old cigar box.

VICTORIA FORD Our living room bookshelves are predominantly filled with Harry Potter books. We're big fans, but that's not why we have them. We hunted for a ton of copies before our wedding and gave them away as party favors. But all of the ones that were left, we kept. So now we always have this fun decorative reminder of one of the best days of our lives. And the older we get, the more spills the copies get and the more pages that come out of them, and they just keep getting better and better. And we find ourselves decorating around them because they are such a part of the fabric of our lives now.

TESSA FOLEY I have a small corner gallery wall in this room filled with artwork collected on trips to New England—Cape Cod, Boston, Nantucket. I have several pieces of scrimshaw art from a Nantucket artist I discovered at the weekly summer farmer's market; an oil painting from a favorite art gallery in Cape Cod that is located in a barn next to the general store I used to visit while vacationing when I was young; and a gorgeous antique seascape bought on a winter girls' trip to Nantucket, from my favorite antique store on the island, where they served lobster bisque and champagne while we were shopping.

90

4

Dining Room

I WONDER at what point in the life cycle of a family the dining room becomes a place simply to eat meals. For families in a certain season of life, in the throes of business-building and child-rearing, the dining room wears many hats. Ours is the place where we eat, but it's also the place where we begin sketches for design plans, and the place where diapers are changed on the antique oak buffet. This is the contradictory situation in which growing families with smallish houses find themselves. The dining room is both museum and café. It is where we conduct toddler art class with tempera paint; it's the dinner table and chairs that, when draped with a blanket, double as Helen's clubhouse; and someday it will be where she stares at high school algebra, a fog settling around her brain, with her mother's inability to understand the language of numbers. We live in every inch of our home but especially in the dining room, where only some of my memories include meals.

Before it was ours, it was a formal dining room, all polished walnut and cabriole legs. A place to eat lunch in your Sunday clothes. It was easily transformed into a more casual room with Dover White paint and an antique wingback upholstered in a blue-striped flour sack. The first piece of furniture Ben built for this house was the dinner table, which I have fond attachments to, even with its primitive joinery and finishes. It was only the second thing he ever built, and he wishes we could throw it in a dumpster but I won't allow it. It is special. In apartments you eat around two-seater hand-me-downs and coffee tables. But this is what growing up means: keeping your thermostat on seventy-two in the summer and inviting people over to eat on not-paper plates.

As we were settling into our new home, my parents tore the old back porch off their early-nineties home to build a newer, bigger place for Ole Miss football watch parties. Ben used those porch pieces to build a tabletop eight feet long and three and a half feet wide, big enough to accommodate eight people and a lazy Susan, if I choose to get a lazy Susan someday. When my parents replaced their wooden front porch columns that same summer, Daddy piled them in the backyard shed "just in case." Ben did not yet own a lathe in 2011, so they made fine, sturdy table legs just as they were. Maximum stability, minimum work. All furniture must pass rigorous Napier testing: we must know if it can offer the support and strength to endure regular use by giants of Scottish ancestry. You might think eating at the table would be a good enough test, but Ben stood on it and bounced a little to see if the legs would sway at the joints. It made a settling creak but did not move, so it passed muster.

After it was finished, I asked how hard it would be for the novice woodworker to add drawers for cloth napkin storage and to provide a little dimension and hardware. Hard, as it turns out. And so, he made false drawer fronts and attached them to the skirt, and my guests were none the wiser. We collected uncomfortable but fashionably early American ladder-backs and rush-bottoms from flea markets and estate sales for twenty dollars each and felt we overpaid. Until we saw what dinner chairs cost in catalogs. And then we decided to sit happily at our dinner table in our pack of feral seating, smugly pointing it out to our friends: got this pretty chair for a steal! This is what you do when you're young, scrappy homeowners. You date middling furniture for a few years, until you find the more stable piece you want to marry. There are pieces of furniture you might find in a flea market for a bargain that remain with you your entire life, heirlooms to pass down. Other pieces don't evolve with you, and the time comes to let them go to another home. Once Helen was toddling,

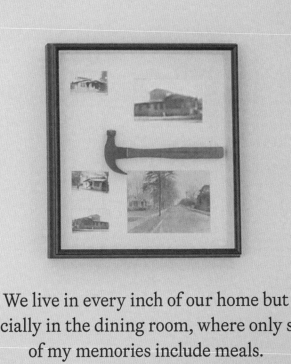

We live in every inch of our home but especially in the dining room, where only some of my memories include meals.

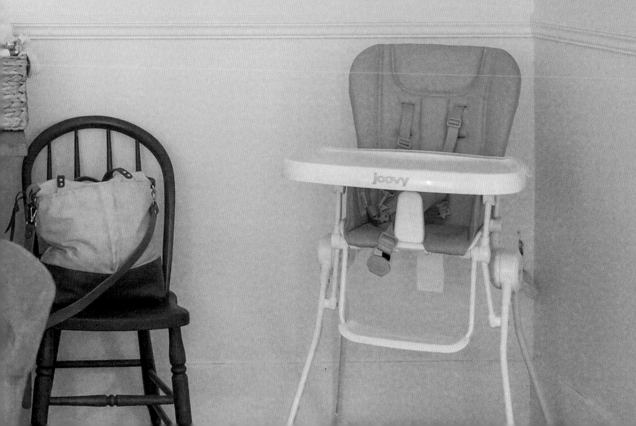

grasping for balance on every piece of furniture in the house, we found that our top-heavy flea market chairs became a liability and realized we could now actually afford to replace them with better, sturdier ones that wouldn't tip and terrify Mama.

There is art in our dining room, but it serves as a conversation starter most of all. The art in the other rooms of our house feels apropos, singing with the spirit of that room's use. Food art in the kitchen. Our family history in the entry, like a welcome wagon. Figural sketches and Walter Anderson calendar prints from our birthdays in the bedroom. But the dining room is where we sit for hours, where conversation is lively and scattered, where the room's purpose is not clearly defined. And so the art reflects that wabi-sabi, tongue-in-cheek way we use it. It is collected, unusual, and there is one painting we adore that seems an unorthodox choice only if you recognize its truth. Those who've never spent an hour enraptured by our favorite New Jersey crime family don't recognize the oil portrait of a man toasting with champagne, standing regally beside a brown racehorse in a field, as the painting of Tony Soprano and Pie-O-My from the series. My aunt Mae saw it and declared, "That's Ben's daddy. And his horse," and we did not correct her. Just as well, seeing as we live in the Bible Belt. Beside Tony is Helen's first scribble in blue and red crayon—a masterpiece of fine motor skills, framed in gold. Above the teak and glass china cabinet, below a brass picture light, is the oil portrait of Champ, my daddy's English pointer, mid-point on a quail hunt in the autumn woods. Champ died in 1987, but Daddy loved him enough to commission a painting of him, though eventually it was relegated to the tiny family cabin in the woods and forgotten. And then I stole it and hung it in our dining room. And then Daddy asked where I got it and said he wanted it back. But finders keepers. A World War II Red Cross poster and the sea-tattered American flag with thirteen stars Ben found on a garage shelf at an estate sale for two dollars flank French doors to the living room. The flag looks to be of historical significance, though we do not know what it is. It was machine-made, and so a pre–World War I replica flag as best we can tell, but it is easy to eat a meal beneath it and feel like you might be in the presence of Revolutionary War history.

We finished the first renovation of our house in the spring of 2012 and invited our families over for a two-part Easter weekend. Ben's parents and his siblings and their families came on Saturday so his minister parents could be at church on Sunday, and Sunday involved the greater Rasberry and Walters clan: my parents, my brother and his family, and my grandmother, great-aunt, cousins, aunts, and uncles. We set up a card table beside the porch dinner table to make more room, and still some of us ate off our laps sitting on the low-slung porch walls. It was the first time to show off the fruits of our six-month labor, and for a few years, Easter became our event. The best Easters included my cousin Kent, a Baptist music minister with a gold cross on a chain and gently feathered hair, ready to lead some light worship with a Gaither band knee-slapper. He is honest as the day is long, and that first Easter after blessing the meal he told us about having the gall to tell off the drug dealers in a rough part of town where he'd just bought an old fixer-upper to renovate and house his antique furniture collections. After he gave them a talking-to, they never left their trash cans out by the sidewalk all week again. Then we cut the coconut cake.

As our brothers' and cousins' families grew, we outgrew Easter lunch at our house. When Helen was first born, she had her bottles in that wingback chair, then ate her first spoonful of sweet potatoes at the table her daddy built; then finally the vacant high chair in the corner had a job to do. When she outgrew it, I did not know the last time I pulled her out of it would be the last time. Weeks later, deep-cleaning her crumbs from the cracks and crevices of the seat cushion, as its season was over, I had to stop myself from crying. Now she tells everyone where they will sit at our table for a meal, so long as she has the best spot: in the middle chair, atop her booster cushion. For two years, the high chair sat sentinel in the corner, waiting for Mae to have the core strength needed to eat a spoonful of mashed lima beans. I'm grateful to once again have the duty of cleaning up the confetti of toddler mealtime on the floor underneath the high chair.

One morning, after I changed her diaper, before her morning bottle, Mae lay on her back, marveling at Tony Soprano and his horse as she does every morning. I'm realizing I will soon have to make room for her on these walls too, maybe the first time she picks up a paintbrush and makes a bold swipe across paper. ✪

> I'm grateful to once again have the duty of cleaning up the confetti of toddler mealtime on the floor underneath the high chair.

ALY SMITH Eating our first meal after we moved into our house is a big memory. We had this really tiny dinner table from our small house in Memphis and picked up pizza after a long day at work. Just sitting there realizing we had this dream come true of a house and we could fill it with all the things that mattered most to us and hopefully one day the kids we've dreamed of. It was an overwhelming feeling of relief to know we'd finally found a landing spot.

BRIAN PATRICK FLYNN My dining room is actually just an oddly shaped space below a sloping ceiling. To put it to good use, I added a four-seater sofa along the back wall and a round pedestal table. Out of ideas for what to place on the wall, I remember my husband and I just trying out all of the resin antlers and randomly placing them to break up all the rigid angles of the walls. We eyeballed it all and it seemed like total chaos at the time, but the end result looks awesome, and I love how we did it together.

Home Town, Season 5

THE DAVIS-JEFCOAT HOUSE

One of the hallmarks of the work we do on *Home Town* is using
as much as we can of what the house gives us. Brooke and Robbie's house gave
us brown shag carpet, which was an easy discard, but it also gave us
the dining room's deep, dark feminine wallpaper from the early 1990s that
somehow still felt fresh and timeless. Since we would not modify
doorways in that room, it gave us the option to use that floral wallpaper and
build a rich and intimate dining room color story around it. I knew
Brooke when she was in her early twenties, with this alternative
emo flavor about her style, and I felt it brought that piece of who she has
always been into the design of their house.

—ERIN

BROOKE DAVIS-JEFCOAT   When Kingston brings art home from school we tape it in the window to display it because they look the prettiest when the sun settles in behind the trees at the end of the day. He brings every new guest over to his art display window and shows them his newest creation. It feels cozy and warm, yet a bit romantic on an evening when Mom and Dad get to have dinner alone.

CAT BUDE The dining room is a gathering space. That room started out as a library, and we called it that even after adding a table (many tables). Initially we ran my business from that room as well. We would take out all of the chairs and store them upstairs, and we would squeeze in as many tables as we possibly could to spread out orders, wrap, and ship all of the purchases from my online shop. We called it our "flex" room, as we would set it up and break it down each month for two weeks at a time. We literally had packing materials stacked to the ceiling, and my husband's desk was crammed into a small space in the corner. But I loved that room—it was always quiet. And I dreamed of a time when we could have a huge table, and candles lit, and host amazing dinners with friends we had yet to meet. Several years ago we took on a warehouse "atelier," and now our work operations and inventory are over there and the room is permanently set as a dining room. I finally got my three-meter-long dining table that seats twelve, and the fireplace mantel is always set with stacks of books and candles. There is a bar table in the corner, and glasses always ready, and in the corner is now a leather wing chair where you can sit with a book and a glass of something.

JENNIFER FAITH The dining room is a great room for working puzzles on the big table. I also love all my cookbooks in there. It is nice to grab a book and drink a cup of coffee and read.

LINDA CARSON Making essential-oil bath salts and sugar scrubs at the dining room table with our daughter and our daughter-in-law are some of my favorite memories.

MALLORIE RASBERRY   The history of this house pulled us in and we had to have it. We wanted to know for certain that this piece of Laurel history was preserved and loved. Sometimes I like to playfully think of this house as my third child. Much like Lucy and Lottie, we hope we mold her and give her the best shot at success so she can grow old(er) and pass down the stories, all while creating amazing new memories in between. She's got a lot of life left to live, so we hope we are good stewards for the next generation.

PATTI WAGNER Pre-kids, we meticulously taped off the glass so we could enamel the two built-ins in the dining room. We'd both come home late from work, have dinner, and start working on the house. I don't have bad memories of those early renovation days even if there were challenges, only how we bonded to make this home ours.

TESSA FOLEY The antique harvest dining room table was an estate sale find that we had to squeeze into the back of a borrowed truck to bring home. It's where we eat most of our meals, where homework is done, where I wrap Christmas gifts and my kids complete school projects, where I set up my sewing machine on the rare occasions I attempt to sew something, and where we host friends and family. It's where we sing to celebrate birthdays and toast life's milestones, where Charlie sat to eat his first cupcake and where Andrew sat when he submitted his college applications. There are indentations from essays and math homework, and water rings from glasses. So much life happens around this table.

5

Bedroom

THERE ARE two personalities on display in our bedroom: my side of the bed, and Ben's side of the bed. The night we married, we drew the property lines and never changed them again. I have felt and always will feel the furnace heat and safety of Ben sleeping by my left arm. He will forever be propping on his right elbow for the last kiss before sleep, wrestling the tiredness of a day spent on his feet, building beautiful things. Our nightstands, antique dressers from the last century, explain who we are.

I am three stacks of books, each six inches tall. The bottom book, *Streams in the Desert*, and my two journals—one to record three sentences about events of the day, one to remember the things our babies have said, their exact child phrasing and created words—and a pencil are the only constants of them all. I am a small blue-and-white porcelain dish with a lid to hide the lip balm and earplugs. I am a clip-on reading light that has color and dimness options. I am an ambitious homebody who travels the world through the pages of books. I am orderly. I document. I remember.

Ben is a stack of books about the history of the screwdriver, the history of road trips in America, the Bible, early American furniture joinery, a biography of the bourbon-making Van Winkle family splayed open on its pages so he doesn't lose his place. He doesn't believe in dog-earing a page. He is three catchalls, each overflowing with a tangled heap of keys with no locks, pocketknives, broken aviator sunglasses, ticket stubs from a Duke basketball game, a spent coffee cup and a Mason jar of water, our backstage lanyards from seeing Chris Stapleton, a Duke University pencil sharpened with a knife so often it is now two inches long, handkerchiefs that seem clean but are crumpled, so I leave them. He is a Bush Dairy glass milk bottle full to the brim with pocket change, a small piece of tiger maple broken from a piece of furniture he intends to repair (someday). He is a business card that can't be discarded. Ben loves people, learning about them, and loves working. It is what boys do, work with their hands, with sticks and toy trucks. His pocket collections that are laid out on his dresser at the end of the day would make boy Ben proud of man Ben, that he did not abandon the pursuits of boyhood in favor of office work.

Our bedrooms are our private places, where we do our storing and burrowing. It's where the baby box with a lock of hair from Helen's first haircut is tucked under the bed; it's the blanket chest where we keep love letters and old photographs, the drawer where the socks and underwear live. In my mother's bedroom, in an accordion folder inside a nightstand, beside her and Daddy's last wills and testaments and the birth certificates for my brother and me, is a copy of Elvis Presley's death certificate. We are southern and we have reverence for our idols. We get dressed and undressed and try a different pair of pants and model them in the mirror, satisfied enough with the look of things to head to work. Other things happen in bedrooms too, but this is not that kind of book.

Photos of my bedroom often appear on Pinterest alongside captions like "Best Farmhouse Ideas," and I feel a bit deflated at the mislabeling of my craftsman house that's very much in town, but there are worse insults. When we moved in, we painted the walls Dover White and got blackout roller shades and hung the canvas curtains my mama lovingly sewed for us. We bought an antique-style metal bed, queen-size to fit the room, but also so we wouldn't be spoiled for traveling. You never know when you'll be sharing a king or a queen on the road. We found a cedar blanket chest with the initials of some World War II soldier carved into it at a flea market and painted the outside fatigue green, but even three cans of coffee and a carbon filter could not erase the smell of decades of mothballs inside, so we never placed a blanket in it. I found small lamps that looked like ginger jars with ivory shades, and remembered a childhood friend's elegant mother once saying, "Every beautifully

designed room must have a moment of chinoiserie." The hulking pine armoire, the first piece of furniture Ben built when we lived in our loft, was still his only option for a closet so it came with us, calling the shots on where all the other furniture would land. And because we live in perpetual summer in Mississippi, I chose a linen duvet and percale sheets that would be cool to sleep under, even in January. I tore two pages from my college newsprint sketchbook with charcoal figure drawings and framed them to hang from the picture rails on either side of the bed.

The light of the ginger jar lamps is the finish line of the day in my mind's eye. While turning them off, I take stock of who I have been that day, what I have accomplished. The year I turned thirty, I began to feel the urgency of growing our family but was paralyzed by fear of how it would change me, change our relationship, our life. I would read until midnight, then turn out the light and sigh: another day had passed and I was still not brave enough to attempt motherhood. It felt like a promotion I would never get for a job I didn't know if I was equipped to do. Then one night in May 2017, I turned out the light with relief as an expecting mother. I had gotten the job. Whether I would excel at it was yet to be seen, but there was comfort in just knowing it was happening whether I was ready for it or not.

Both of our babies spent their early months in a bassinet by the bed, until the sun would wake us before crying did; when they were old enough, they made the move to the nursery upstairs. It happens so quickly, the days bleeding into weeks, until one day they are no longer soft helpless bundles in danger of rolling off the edge of a bed. Just days later, they're lean and sinewy and have lost the rolls at their wrists, jumping on the bed and wet from the bathtub, riding the last wave of adrenaline before sleep claims them in their twin beds upstairs.

Those early weeks of life with babies, the bedroom is the center of it. The sleepless nights and feedings, the diaper changes, the day you close the bedroom door and weep in private, away from the baby, because you wonder if you'll ever be rested enough to feel like yourself again. But you do. You become yourself again, feeling wiser and stronger than you used to be, with new tiny people who look a little like you and a little like him, falling in step with this new dance you're choreographing.

Now the lamp is no longer my finish line. When the light goes out, I click from standby to the electric blue glow of the baby monitor and look in on them. I see them breathing and dreaming, their little faces just two among the stuffed puppies and bears, and then I know that for today, I was good enough. ✤

Our bedrooms are our
private places,
where we do our storing
and burrowing.

BRIAN PATRICK FLYNN (ABOVE) The bedroom is more or less a converted attic, and what I love most about it is how cozy it feels. Due to all of the odd angles in the space, I chose a plaid wallpaper to make them disappear, and the pattern reminds me of a classic Icelandic knit sweater, one I bought on my first trip there in December of 2015.

KARA PHILLIPS (OPPOSITE) The oil painting on Brett's side table is of his great-grandfather. There is something wonderful about heritage and family heirlooms that remind you of the past and how characteristics pass between generations. We treasure this one-of-a-kind painting.

PORTRAITS OF HOME | DISC INTERIORS

TERENCE
CONRAN THE ESSENTIAL HOUSE BOOK

CASSIDY COMPTON When I walked into this room and saw the deep-blue hand-painted floral wallpaper, I knew even more that I was in love with this house. It's dark and moody and so beautiful. I said that this wallpaper looked like it walked out of my dreams. It is old and well taken care of, and I deeply appreciate its existence in my home. I was fine having a tiny little closet. I was fine that it wasn't the room with an attached bath. I just wanted this romantic wallpaper room to be ours.

CAT BUDE This house is a haven, a safe place to rest. We have become the kind of people who prefer to vacation at home. Honestly, given the opportunity to spend a night in Paris or sleep in my own bed, I would choose being at home. As crazy-busy as our life is, it's still comforting and satisfying to host friends here rather than go out to a restaurant, to watch a movie on the couch over going to the cinema.

LAUREN NAPIER If we ever moved, I would always miss our dark bedroom walls, the creak in the door to Nell's room that lets her know we are coming in to get her—the way she immediately starts smiling before we say anything.

ERICA SWAGLER If I had to pick a room that feels the most like me, it would be our bedroom. The patterned wallpaper, antique wooden dresser, blue-and-white curtains— all feel homey and cozy. The wool braided rugs were handmade by my grandma Ann and add to the cozy, homey atmosphere.

LAYLA QUILICHINI-ROVIRA I thrifted the vintage floral mirror in our bedroom for seven dollars and it was painted in a burgundy shade. I decided to get creative with it and transformed it into one of my favorite pieces in our home. Art doesn't have to be perfect. Sometimes I flip the mirror to the back side to enjoy the art I created on it.

LOUISE COSTER Sam and I designed our home together. He worked as a theater designer and I was a fashion designer, so we both have a background in art and design. We work with many interior designers and architects, advising them how to use reclaimed items in their projects.

RENA REGISTER The old iron bed was in one of the barns on our family property. I redid it and it now lives on in this house. My grandfather was a collector of old items, and this bed was in his collection. Also, some personal items of my great-grandmother's are in the bedroom: the clock by the bedside, and a small bird print hanging on the wall.

TESSA FOLEY

I love our bedroom and miss it when
we travel. The interior design was inspired
by charming inns found in New England.
I put climbing into our cozy bed, made up
with freshly washed sheets, with a good
book and a huge mug of tea, right at the
top of life's greatest pleasures.

SANDRA M. CAVALLO If we ever moved, I would miss the incredible sunsets with shades of purple and pink and intense orange that paint the inside of my house. The hydrangeas that take over the yard in the summertime and the iceberg roses climbing along the fence. Watching my kids grow up on the water, sailing and exploring and collecting seashells and sea glass. Knowing the history of this home from its inception and being so intimate with every inch, leaving would be hard but loving our memories will bring joy.

137

6

Guest Room

OUR GUEST rooms change as our families do. They are the most flexible members of the house, evolving from guest quarters to home office to nursery to bedroom to sewing room in the seasons of a family's life, from singledom to family to the empty nest. The rooms where guests have slept in the decade we have owned our house exist on the second story, up high among the oak trees and jasmine vines, but they are not guest rooms now. For a short time, one room held the metal bed my grandparents once slept in as newlyweds,

about a foot too small for Ben's six-foot-four baby brother, Jesse, who would spend the night as a college freshman. More recently it is the room where I've rocked my babies and photographed each one on the monthly anniversary of her birth during her first year of life.

At the top of the steep flight of stairs is a small bookcase, handmade from quartersawn white oak by Ben, perched below the center window of the upstairs. There you can choose the small room on the left or the larger room on the right, both sharing a little bathroom that joins them at the back of our house, making a circle. In 1925, when the house was built, these rooms were unfinished but ready to accommodate a growing family if the need arose, and at some point in the middle of the twentieth century they were insulated and plastered and finished. We painted them Dover White to keep them neutral and brought in two antique beds: both metal, one three-quarter-size (a size that only existed for tiny people in the 1940s, apparently), the other queen-size. We were thrilled to have TWO guest rooms where we could invite friends from far and wide to stay, never mind that the friends we would want to see that badly already lived here in Laurel. So mostly they stood empty, except when Ben's brothers or parents came to town long enough to spend the night. The best guest quarters are constantly anticipating, ready to welcome an overnight guest with comfortable linens and pillows, a thoughtfully chosen book on the nightstand. But one day, the anticipation changes. The focus shifts from an overnight guest to an occupant. The objects and furnishings become more meaningful, heirloom, but ever changing.

When we found out Helen was on the way, we moved the three-quarter bed to storage to make way for a baby girl. I painted the walls the deep, dark color of a mossy stone, and we hung crewelwork flowers embroidered on curtain panels over blackout wooden blinds, planning for good sleep from the night we brought her home. We found an antique bleached pine dresser from France for her changing table, a chambray upholstered rocking chair and footstool, antique botanicals that we framed and latched to the wall in a gallery of plexiglass (for her safety!) above the crib, sconces to keep the light low for bedtime reading, and an antique Turkish rug in shades of green and peach beneath her crib, leaving room for the most important piece of the puzzle: the quartersawn white oak crib Ben built. It had bobbin turnings for feet, and a small piece of heart pine in the center rail that came from a stud wall inside our house: a piece of her childhood home that would be part of her own someday, when her babies sleep inside that same passed-down heirloom crib. We rocked each night at bedtime in the corner by the windows, with the man in the moon watching through the wavy glass as we prayed the prayer our mamas taught us:

Now I lay me down to sleep
I pray the Lord my soul to keep
Guide me safely through the night
And wake me with the morning light
Amen.

The objects and furnishings become more meaningful,
heirloom, but ever changing.

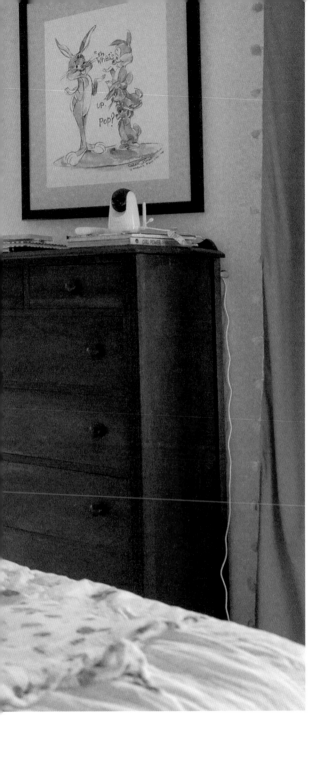

The morning a hailstorm crashed into Laurel, I ran up the stairs at 5 a.m. and snatched Helen from the crib and carried her downstairs as she whimpered, and I prayed the ice was not as strong as those hundred-year-old windows that had seen Camille and Katrina bring down mighty oaks and pecans all around our house. We didn't find a single crack in the panes, though the two-year-old roof had to be replaced. They really don't make things like they used to.

As the people who inhabit the rooms of a house mature, so do the rooms themselves. They cannot remain static without stifling who we are becoming. There was no pink in the nursery when Helen was born, because babies do not care what colors their rooms are. Little girls do, though, and when Helen turned three she was ready to move into the bigger room across the stair landing. She asked for dark-blue walls and ballerina bedding, and we compromised. I gave her the bedding but kept the walls white, because Mama was tired of painting rooms. We found a pair of matching antique mahogany Reid Classics pencil-post twin beds built by the grandfather of Ben's dear friend and mentor Andrew Reid. After an inspection and shine-up by Andrew, we moved them in and added antique prints of ballerinas and trapeze artists from the 1920s, a pink and turquoise

Turkish rug between them, and a double sconce for bedtime reading.

For weeks before Helen made the move out of the nursery, we began to practice. We would read books in her new mahogany big-girl bed before bringing her back to the crib to sleep for the night. Between the last two verses of "Let's Call the Whole Thing Off," her favorite bedtime lullaby, I reminded Ben we needed to engrave this in our memory, to let it leave an imprint: we would only sing to her in her crib a few more nights and then it would be the last time. We were grateful for the inky darkness, hiding from Helen that we cried through the last verse, our voices catching on *"For we know we need each other / So we better call the calling off off."*

She never once tried to climb out of the crib; one day when we asked her, "Are you ready to sleep in your big-girl bed or do you want to stay in your crib?" she just answered honestly: "I'm ready to be a big girl, Mama."

And so the nursery, without a baby to cradle in the night, was just a room again.

A guest room. An empty place in our house. I kept the curtains drawn and closed the door.

In May 2020, my grandmother left her earthly body and flew away at age ninety-seven. She left behind two sons and three grandchildren: me, my brother Clark, and my cousin Jim. At her funeral, held in the time of COVID quarantines, a handful of the people who loved her most gathered around her grave on a sun-washed late spring day. We hung back and gave my daddy and his brother, Danny, some space to be alone with her before the casket was closed. These two grown men, with more differences than commonalities, leaned into one another. They fortified one another. They looked on her face, at peace, and found a peace of their own. I watched them and felt a lurch in my stomach at the thought of our own inevitable future: *When I am the one in the grave, who will stand over me? Will Helen cry with a husband to comfort her, but no one who remembers the way her father wrote me letters every morning before I woke up? No one who knows what his cedar closet smelled like, or the way I made lasagna without first boiling the pasta? If no one is there to share those memories, what happens when one loses them?*

After lunch one afternoon in May, a few days after my grandmother's funeral, I was folding laundry on the dining table. Helen was napping, and Ben was reading on the back porch. I was alone, except for the portrait of Helen at age two, her curious stare and a curl behind her ear, watching me. Above the portrait is a landscape of cold blue hills beside a placid lake. I idly thought of how alone her portrait was, hanging there, with no other faces beside it. Weeks before, I had taken the changing pad and basket that once held diapers from atop the oak buffet up to the closet in the guest room. As I folded our underwear and dresses and shirts, the buffet beside me now held a wooden tray of rolled cloth napkins, offering me no comfort as I ached for the duties of new motherhood, of changing diapers and burping. My baby was a girl now, and alone, without a sibling to share her books, her dreams, her snacks. As she slept in her big-girl bed, across the landing was a dark and empty room with no life inside, no companion for our daughter as she wrestled with the world and the hardships it would deal her.

I did not want a guest room. I wanted a nursery again.

Now our life feels like we've hit rewind and it is 2018 again, in many ways. There is a tiny blond-haired, blue-eyed baby girl who sleeps in the crib in the green room with the crewelwork curtains. She slept through the night from five weeks old, beating her older sister by one week, and in that way God is merciful on us older parents who are quickly approaching the top of the hill. She is a good and predictable baby, who only cries for a bottle and squeezes our necks so tightly as she quietly coos, "Ohhh. Ohhh," into our ears, her sweet milk and nothing breath imprinted

I did not want a guest room. I wanted
a nursery again.

in my memory forever. Chris Stapleton signed Helen's toy cowboy guitar with this message: "Helen, snuggle your parents!" with no result. Much as we crave her affection, Helen is like a cat, uninterested in snuggles, but tolerating the occasional scratch on her back. But Mae cuddles, she nestles in and makes your chest feel the way it feels to hear the good part of your favorite song. Mae is her father in this way, greeting every person she meets with a warm, close embrace. She adores her sister and watches her closely, learning how to be a little person. While Helen is the dancer and musician of the two, Mae is the singer. She jabbers along with the songs we listen to, almost in tune already, though she is

still only an infant! I daydream of them starting a sister garage band when they become teenagers. Mae folds her soft hand into a tiny fist and holds it up to her ear, an imaginary telephone, and says, "Hello!" We squeal with delight, telling ourselves the story that no baby has ever been so advanced. She turns her head to the right and closes her eyes tight as she stretches in the morning when I open the curtains, and grins with her open mouth at the sight of Helen, or me or her daddy. I rock her in the chambray chair and we read *Goodnight Moon*.

Someday maybe I will teach myself to quilt or scrapbook in that room.

But not today. ✹

AMANDA WATTERS Our boys' shared room is a playful, nostalgic space that reflects our love of primitive New England style, with a more modern approach. It specifically nods to a trip our family of six took last summer to Nantucket, where we gathered heaps of design inspiration for our new home, and a sailboat or two for decoration. A simple thrift store cot is wrapped in an antique wool throw I found at an estate sale, one of my hobbies, and is a great option for sleepovers, as it can easily be stored under a bed. And there's always a dinosaur or two dueling on the rug nearby.

Our home is full of antiques and secondhand items, like our little one's nursery with this gorgeous English pine bed, handmade grain-sack quilt, Shaker bedside table, and darling wool sheep. It gives me joy not only living with pieces that have been previously loved on in other homes by other families but also knowing that we are treading a bit lighter on the earth by using secondhand items in our everyday life as opposed to buying new, new, new. My very favorite homes are ones that have been collected with care over time. They sing a comforting song to me.

150

CASSIDY COMPTON   My favorite memory here is listening to their dad reading them bedtime stories. He is always reading them a new chapter book, and it is such a peaceful way to end a day. This room is shared by my two youngest sons. We don't have a ton of toys in here, but we keep the toys we play with most. I love the sound of wood blocks being stacked and how the deep-green walls make us feel like we could be playing in a forest.

LAUREN NAPIER The guest room has housed many friends and family for weekend stays. It has the best morning light, so I always take Nell in there and let her play while I paint at the desk, which is from Jesse's parents' house.

EMILY SAXTON   We always knew this room would be the perfect nursery. We hoped and prayed to fill this room with a child, and in the perfect timing, we found out we were expecting and started thinking of how the room would look. I chose to put mostly family artwork—floral watercolors done by my sister and a floral watercolor and some landscape watercolor paintings done by my precious grandmother, Mary Jane, who we named our baby girl (Jane) after. I wanted to tell Jane about her through the artwork on the walls and be constantly reminded of what a gift I had in her namesake and what a gift this child was to us. The old pink-tiled bathroom attached even reminds me of one similar in my grandparents' house. Now we spend so much time in this room. Memories of rocking her as a newborn in the chair and us piled in here eating breakfast or whatever meal picnic-style on the floor to be together while I fed her, now watching as she crawls all over the room and plays with her books and toys. When I look in the room, I'm reminded of what a blessing family is, and the many stories that have been read and the many songs than have been sung in here.

LOUISE COSTER

JENNIFER FAITH   The spare bedroom is another favorite room. I love the wallpaper, along with the built-in bookshelves that I have tried to make into a cabinet of curiosities. My husband painted that for me, so it is special to me. Some of my favorite old oil paintings are in there as well. I always do my Christmas wrapping in the spare bedroom so I can spend more time in there!

LEIGH MULDROW   Upstairs, the bedrooms are not large, but I have always made a point since our kids were little to keep most of their toys in another space so their bedrooms could easily feel tidy and relaxing. Ella is our youngest child; her room also happens to be the smallest, with the most challenging storage situation. Ben and I recently added all the wall trim and peg rail to give her some more space to display things and hang her favorite stuffies in a basket on the wall rather than having them piled up on the floor. She loves the Vera the Mouse books by Marjolein Bastin, so her room is definitely inspired by Marjolein's illustration style, with a little punch of bright yellow to suit Ella's vibrant personality. I hope she looks back and thinks of her childhood bedroom as if it could have been out of a storybook.

LINDA PHAN SCOTT This room feels very much like a boutique hotel, and we love setting guests up in here! Although we once had our nephew stay in here and he didn't enjoy it—he was scared of all the birds, especially the ostrich lamps! When he left, we found a handful of Lego pieces lying around, including a Batman Lego minifigure on the base of the "scary" bird lamp. We kinda love it when guests accidentally leave little things behind. It's like we get a chance to reunite them with it when they visit next.

PATTI WAGNER   All three of our babies called this their nursery. It holds a lot of precious memories. The tired nights rocking and singing to them—those sleep-deprived nights are just special memories now. We styled this room with many items from Brian's childhood. It's so fun to see Brian share with our kids about each item, like the books he wrote or the old Fisher-Price toys he played with.

MALLORIE RASBERRY   Man, I love a good antique piece of furniture with a story . . . but even more than that, I love a good deal! I found these old beds in an estate sale and recognized immediately that they must have an incredible story. Turns out, they are out of a United States Navy cargo ship from World War II. After the war, the ship was no longer needed and then dismantled . . . BUT these beds were saved from the captain's quarters. I got both beds for ninety dollars total (they may honestly be my best bargain to date)! We cleaned them up, repaired where needed, and added trim around because I wanted them to feel as if they were built-ins, original to the house. I love them so much. I don't even mind that I nearly throw my back out every time I make the beds.

7

Bathroom

MY FIRST trip to the brand-new mall in Hattiesburg was in 1994, when my mother took me to a bath store and let me choose my own bubble bath. Plumeria was the scent, and "Hook" by Blues Traveler was on the radio on the drive home as I considered all the very grown-up things my future held as a now grown-up who chose my very own grown-up bubble bath. I bounded up the stairs to my room and drew a bath and discarded my clothes along with childish things because I was going to soak and "relax." With great reverence, I poured a ribbon of the pearlescent pink syrup under the rush of water and watched the white bubbles float to the surface, and then I climbed into them. I was in fifth grade, and I had found the delicious experience of bath form vs. bath function, and it became an offering of comfort as much as a way to come clean.

Even now as a grown woman, when I need comfort I want one of these things: Ben's arms around me, a grilled cheese sandwich, a phone call with my mom, or a long soak in the bath.

When we married, Ben took what he knew about me and made those tenets of our relationship. In our drafty old flatiron loft, the cast-iron claw-foot tub was my favorite place, and the night we returned home from our honeymoon in late November, he drew a hot bath for me and left the book I'd been reading on the windowsill beside it. I read until the water was cool and sleep was close. The stress of traveling, of the workweek that lay ahead of me, it all felt small. Manageable. I regret that through our newlywed years, I unknowingly suffered from a partially ruptured appendix that stumped doctors all over the Southeast, and a warm bath was the only hope I had when the pain was unbearable. After writhing in the sheets or on the floor to try to relieve the gnawing ache, I found that repeat trips to the bathtub were the only help and comfort. I remember spending four hours in the tub alone in the middle of the night, just draining the cold water and filling it again with warm to keep from crying. In 2014, a surgery removed that wretched thing, and baths became an innocuous, sweet routine again instead of a desperate remedy.

When we found out we were expecting Helen, we had to make a decision about the bathroom of our 1925 craftsman. We could keep it as is, renovated beautifully by the previous owner, but with only one door: into the hallway instead of our room. It was the bathroom of choice for every visitor, and I always felt embarrassed about my hot-pink hair dryer left on the counter, the toilet paper pack sitting unopened in the corner by the toilet. Some things should be private, and the primary bath is one of those things. We added a half bath under the stairs to mitigate the traffic to our bathroom, and the final step would be to close off the door into the hall and reconfigure so it became accessible only from our bedroom. We decided it would be awful to renovate while pregnant and filming ten episodes of *Home Town*, but infinitely worse to do all that with a newborn. So we began an impulsive renovation that took four months because we began demolition on June 29, 2017, before we ordered any of the materials to fill the space. We know now, after years of renovating on television, that to renovate a house in eight weeks, you must have everything you'll need ready to install before you begin tearing it down. For 102 days, while pregnant, tired, and distracted by our work, we renovated. One afternoon in the process of extending one of the bathroom walls, we discovered a hammer, lost in the stud wall in 1925, marked and worn but sturdy and still good for working. Not even an hour later, our doorbell rang; the granddaughter of the Haynes family,

who built our house, was standing on our porch. She seemed embarrassed to show up unannounced but had discovered something buried in a hope chest that she wanted us to have. She handed us a manila envelope of original photos from the week her grandfather, the first dentist in the city of Laurel, finished building the house. It was obvious to us that those objects belonged together, and we had the photos and the hammer shadow-boxed to hang in the dining room.

As the renovation finally came to an end—the walls were painted a deep green, with polished Carrara marble tile rising to shoulder height; the stained-wood medicine cabinets were recessed between brass and milk-glass sconces, above European bleached-pine dressers turned vanities; a freestanding bathtub with a brass faucet sat below the original ninety-year-old windows; and the walk-in shower was finally big enough to accommodate Ben—we were less than three months away from Helen's arrival. I cried with happiness when I eased my pregnant, aching back into the bath for the first time in all those months. For the next few weeks, Ben would bring my pregnancy craving to the tub while I soaked: two Eggo waffles with melted butter and Blackburn's cane syrup, and a glass of grape juice. We know that the reason Helen is so sweet is because she is made of waffles. On January 3, 2018, at 6 a.m., my water broke as I stood in that tub, shaking and scared because it was three weeks earlier than we were expecting. Ben held my hands and helped me out of the tub, then packed his hospital bag and excitedly called our mothers, who knew Helen was coming before he said a word.

Three days later, we were brand-new parents clumsily washing a newborn for the first time in a plastic cradle that was a tub within the tub. She screamed until her face turned the color of an apple, screamed with all her tiny might in terror at the splashing and the cold air above the warm water. Just days later, she is a lanky, skinny swimmer who mastered swim school and is creating underwater worlds with plastic mermaids, her head staying beneath the surface as she measures out her breath, making a hairpin turn like a very large eel in a very small aquarium. As I put on my makeup and dry my hair each morning, she is scaling the vanity to explore the treasures of my jewelry armoire, the rings with turquoise stones, the gold charms in the shape of her own silhouette. She loses interest after applying my blush to her cheeks, and then she is in the bathtub, swimming, swimming, for as long as we will leave her. Already, she knows the secret of how a bath can change us, make our mood sunnier.

I know that the temperature is exactly where Helen prefers it only when the tub-filler handle is pointing straight ahead. Daddy doesn't know this, and Helen can look at it and tell he has run the bath a bit too hot, pointed just south of parallel. At night, she climbs in again and together we bathe Mae, who giggles as we wash her, the little rolls of her legs, the folds around her neck and ears, the creamy baby-wash bubbles between her toes. Helen can't stop herself from kissing her sister, her hands, her feet, the top of her fuzzy head. She tells her someday she will show her how to play mermaid games, how to swim without floaties.

Mae babbles sweetly back, for she is made from toasted strawberry Pop-Tarts, which I nibbled like a delicacy in the bathtub while Helen splashed around my feet, my belly rising from the water, a submarine for her mermaid friends to climb. ✤

ANTHONY D'ARGENZIO   When I walk into this room I am reminded of the evolution of [my company] Zio and Sons—I was so excited to use my debut tile collection with Clé to complete the space, and it turned out just the way I imagined.

CASSIDY COMPTON
In this room I think of all the bath-time evenings with our children. I hear the splashing of toys and feel our kids heavy in my arms as I lift them out of the claw-foot tub wrapped in soft towels. The pink lights and peachy gloss paint warm up this space at night, making it a most magical place for baths.

CAT BUDE Our master bath is actually the only "bathroom" in the house. It has a shower, tub, and sink, and it is used by the entire family. Yes, we share one bathroom, which is only accessible from our bedroom. Typical of European homes, our toilet (again—only one!) is in a small closet in the stairway. The bathroom was a disaster when we moved in. Previously painted orange and navy blue, it had aquatic tiles that featured various fish. We called it the *Finding Nemo* bathroom. But even so, it took two years for us to put it on the top of our priority list for a facelift. We went with a soft gray-beige and white palette and used American-style wainscoting to mend the bad walls and protect the walls around the tub. There is a huge window and amazing light and tall ceilings, and I often pretend it's a private bathroom and not a family one. As I pick up socks and hang damp towels and put away toothbrushes, I am soon back to the "charming" reality.

KEYANNA BOWEN My husband and I spent weeks looking for a rental to no avail. Just when we were about to give up hope, this adorable 1950s Cape Cod–style home came on the market. It was old and dated, which is typically not what you want in a rental, but I've always dreamed of living in a fixer-upper that I could update (even as a renter). I knew this house was "the one" the second I stepped foot inside the door. Most renters wouldn't have been able to look past the dingy kitchen, dated bathrooms, and walls clad with old-fashioned wallpaper, but all I could see was charm, character, and massive potential to put some tender love and care back into this home.

ERICA SWAGLER (ABOVE & MIDDLE)

EMILY JAMES

LAUREN NAPIER

The soaking tub in our
enormous bathroom and
the smudge prints on the
mirror from Nell are the
best things about it.

LOUISE COSTER If we were to ever move, I would most definitely miss the sense of history of this house. It's over five hundred years old, so it's fascinating to think about the families who would have lived here over the years.

RENA REGISTER (ABOVE) I love the direct sunlight. I stand in the window and put my makeup on every morning. And who doesn't love a good pocket door? I love relaxing in my tub. I pretend I'm on vacation sometimes, and then reality tells me that this is my house.

LINDA CARSON (OPPOSITE) While the bathroom may be small, I love the original tile flooring. This was inspiration for the period lighting fixtures.

TESSA FOLEY I don't spend a lot of time in here because I'm pretty low-maintenance when it comes to getting ready and we don't have a bathtub, so it's not a room I linger in. If I had to pick a memory, it would be those times spent getting ready for a special evening or event, when I put a little extra into looking nice and there is still all the anticipation of the evening ahead of us.

VICTORIA FORD We constructed the sink in our bathroom over the span of a couple of years, finding each piece separately and joining them together in the end for a little old and a little new. It's even more special because we installed a similar one in our old house during a really stormy time in our lives before moving a few short weeks later. So we never really got to enjoy it, but this one was created as a joyous response to that one and is just the most wonderful lesson in hope and patience.

8

Office

WHEN WE first set foot inside the yellow cottage, straight ahead in the entry was a door. It was Mrs. Mary Lynn's den. As if the main living room to the left was too cavernous, too much to fill, and not intimate enough for the two of them, she and her husband had their comfortable recliners and a little TV in this small room the color of corn silk, behind a closed door. When it became ours, it was simply a square, blank room for us to project our need onto. We painted the walls Dover White like the rest of the interior; then Ben built frames from old windows and scrap wood to display the maps of places we had traveled together, places of significance to us, and we hung them from the picture rails and stacked them from ceiling to floor, on every inch of the walls. We placed a love seat slipcovered in white denim opposite the entry, and covered the glider Mary Lynn left for us in matching denim, all arranged around a maroon kilim rug. Though I had planned for the first time to separate my work and home lives when we moved out of the loft and into this cottage, I couldn't leave that part of me completely. I needed a desk and a computer, but Mary Lynn was leaving behind the piano in the room for safekeeping until her grandson had a permanent home for it someday, and I was glad of it. If half the room was for music, only half would belong to work—a story I told myself about how I would stop living to work and start working to live. I knew that entrepreneurship had formed unhealthy habits in my life by then. I had goals of working hard and saving ninety cents of every dollar my little company made, but I knew that was stealing my life and time with Ben when it took 90 percent of every waking hour. Music was a transition out of work for me sometimes. I would hear a Ben Folds song I loved from high school, then leave my desk for the piano bench and try to tap it out on the keys from memory. Ten years on, Mrs. Mary Lynn's piano still sits here, with one accidental addition: a water ring from one of Helen's toy teacups. Her grandson just finished college, so I suppose soon I'll be calling my parents about moving my childhood piano to town.

In this room, in its first life as an office, I worked with Ben to organize his campaign for city council and made spreadsheets of volunteers who would help us knock on doors, and it felt like important work: proof that we cared about downtown Laurel more than anyone else. My creativity was boundless. I didn't realize it then, but I had infinite time. My luxury wedding stationery company, Lucky Luxe, was my progeny, my only baby, and I felt its pull at all hours, most especially at night. We were so young, and so free from responsibilities after dinner, and the miles we walked around the neighborhood in the dark were the foundation of our early marriage. Ben and I would talk about everything, leaving nothing unknown to one another. We missed the first twenty years of life together, and there was much to catch up on to learn what had made us who we had become.

After the walks, I would go to my desk, tired, but my mind was electric. I had so many thoughts and ideas for my work, I had to save them before sleep. New ideas for a design, a marketing thought, an email to send, and if I didn't do it then, those opportunities might never return to me and I would forget by morning. When work was finished, I wrote. My journal, "Make Something Good Today," was my daily exercise in practicing gratitude and abundance and optimism. It did not come naturally to me for a very long time, but eventually it became urgent and essential to finishing the day well. Even on the worst days, through tears, I would

write. I typed out words of thanksgiving, even if I did not believe them fully. That oak teacher's desk was my stage, and I performed in silence, until my thoughts and my inbox were empty. I would turn out the lamp on the piano, close the door to our bedroom, soak in the tub, and then sleep until the sun greeted me through the wavy glass, waking me without an alarm. That was our life without children. A self-sustained hustle, romantic talk of life and work, the deep, undistracted sleep of childless people, and late-night visits with our friends and brothers in the office while Phoenix or the Decemberists quietly playing on the computer kept our tempo.

Exactly four people could sit comfortably in this room with a desk chair, a gliding armchair, and a love seat. Often Ben's much younger brother, Jesse, would sleep over while he was an undergrad at the college twenty minutes away, and a perch on the arm of the love seat became sinking into the cushions for a three-hour discussion on our generational differences, his major, his future, our best advice a decade ahead of him in life. I'd met Jesse as a twelve-year-old boy in 2005, but now he was a man and my friend and brother. This is where we really learned about each other, about how much we have in common, our thoughts on religion and friendships and how much he likes Denzel Washington. There were many guests in our office for late-night visits, but these with Jesse are the ones that leave a mark on my memory. I think it's because I never had a younger sibling to impress ideas and help upon and it was new for me, even as the wife of a youth minister who was a frequent listener for confused teenagers navigating high school. Jesse became my real brother in that office that had become a little den, again.

That room was always *becoming*, evolving as we did, as our careers and lives changed. Where once I'd worked late into the night to design rough drafts for wedding stationery, we now had a Skype with a production company interested in putting us on HGTV. Where that Skype happened became the room where we filmed interviews in season one. I did not know the office's final iteration when we bought the house, but by season two we were looking for a place to put a baby swing, a bouncer, a crate of stuffed bunnies and dolls with yellow hair. On the way out of the house in a frenzy at 6 a.m. the morning I went into surprise early labor with Helen, Ben took the last pregnant photo of me standing in the middle of the office, a thick wool turtleneck covering the slightest rise in my abdomen, frightened tears in my eyes. By season three, I was soothing a tired newborn in that slipcovered glider. In my favorite photo of Helen as a baby, she is lying against

Ben's chest in that chair, the size of a kitten in his arms like tree branches. I had only one baby in my life then, and my first baby, the business, was gone. When it ended, I wasn't heartbroken. It was a natural graduation from my youth to becoming a mother. A new life and a new world opening up before me. In the early morning on the way to the hospital to give birth to Mae, Ben stopped me for one last pregnant photo in our office. It is 5 a.m. and I am wearing a light-blue polka-dotted sundress, an easy smile on my face. The next step feels less scary when we've walked there before. In the photo, I am headed to the hospital for my second C-section, and

Mallorie hugs me tight in the doorway before I go, a two-time childbirth veteran herself. She'll be there for Helen when she wakes up a big sister in a few hours.

Today, the crate of bunnies overflows into two more baskets that overflow with little plastic horses and tiaras and Slinkies, a dollhouse and a doctor kit, proof that that baby became the big girl in this house and Mae is the one learning, watching, and growing in the room that became a toy box. My work does not happen here now, not ever. There is quite a lot more to my life now than living to work. There is playing and music and dancing and dolls, the work of childhood. ✪

ALY SMITH If we were to ever move, I would miss the afternoon naps on the music room couch with the sun shining in the windows of the back door. The walls hold so much more than just artwork these days....

ADAM TREST This will always be "the studio I illustrated *The Lantern House* in." Every memory I have of working on that book is tied to the way the light came through the skylights in that room.

AMANDA WATTERS I took a bit of a leap with the brighter color in this attic space, but we wanted it to feel sunshiny up here year-round, so yellow it was! I found a muted mustard [Farrow and Ball's Hay] that ended up being the perfect choice for the trim surrounding the room, and we added paneling everywhere to cozy up the space. It's now one of our favorite rooms in the house, perfect for out-of-town guests and short creative retreats upstairs.

EMILY SAXTON This room has a beautiful big window that gives you a view of the live oak tree in our front yard and the quaint park across the street, and has a random assortment of hand-me-down furniture in it. We keep saying we will get rid of the random furniture, but the quirky pieces just feel like us now. An old blue leather couch that my husband had in his house while growing up, then in his dorm and our other home as well, sits in front of the window. Luna, our puppy, loves to sit and look out this window watching the squirrels in the yard and the neighbors walk by. We joke about her window watching but we also enjoy it as well, and now our daughter, Jane, is very intrigued by the view and loves to stand against the couch to see outside. Here is where we sip our morning coffee most days and have quiet time before we start our day or go to work. Here is where home workouts happen for me or where I plan out my barre classes that I teach. There is an old painting of a ship that we found in my grandparents' home after they passed. So many books and dog toys and now baby toys and burp cloths in this room, and I wouldn't have it any other way.

ANTHONY D'ARGENZIO

201

KARA & BRETT PHILLIPS (ABOVE) We spend so many days here sitting side by side. Our businesses have pivoted, changed, and become new all in this small home office. We've changed too. We started working a lot with Zoom in 2020/2021, and it gave us a new perspective on our home office, as it was the background of so many meetings. Our clients were brought into our homes in a whole new way. Our office feels like a moody and creative space to focus on beautiful and intentional design.

BRIAN PATRICK FLYNN (OPPOSITE) My husband and I actually bought our home on the HGTV series *House Hunters International*, and we pointed out in the episode how we wanted an additional sleeping area for any guests, and the only way to do that was to put this bizarre little corner to good use. It seemed impossible at the time, but it actually worked out great, and every time I'm making up that bed for guests, it takes me back to us coming up with that idea together. We're a good team.

CAROLINE BURKS
I think our best memory in the office was the day that Cory got to leave it—he was sent home to work for almost a year during the pandemic, and while it was the perfect place to work from, it was a huge relief for him to be able to reenter his company's office.

Home Town, Season 2
THE BURKS HOUSE

We sometimes work on homes that have long-standing
emotional connections to friends who were previous owners. In this
case, Caroline and Cory's home was once the Ratcliff home.
Rebecca Ratcliff Patrick, who grew up in the house, was one of my
favorite college teachers and a close friend. We wanted to be
especially sensitive to what it once was as it became the future for the
Burks, and that is sometimes a hard balance to strike. The pink
room that became a masculine and elegant home office stands out in
my memory as one of those moments when I wanted to be careful
not to remove any of the existing millwork in that room, but
instead to alter the personality with color.

—ERIN

CASSIDY COMPTON This little room is where I feel the most creative. One side is the original glass-window cabinets and built-in shelves and is so perfect for storing special dishes and serving-ware. The other side is my desk, where I pin things up on the wall that inspire me and where I keep my art supplies, stationery, and any important documents, like drawings from my sons. I remember sitting on my sewing chair here not knowing what creative thing I wanted to do, but that I wanted to do something. All of a sudden I was painting a simple watercolor portrait of my cousin Audrey. I feel very much myself in this special little room.

ERICA SWAGLER In the "lesson room" there is an art piece done by my mom when she was in her twenties. It's a screen print entitled *Cattails* and there were a total of ten that she printed. I remember growing up we had one framed in our house, and so did my grandma—hers was hung above her ebony grand piano. My mom gifted me an original copy when we moved into this house, and mine hangs above the writing desk in this space.

JENNIFER FAITH The game room has been my son's hangout, and I have fond memories of him being in there with friends playing games and making so much noise! It is also a cozy room to read in. I love the textiles in there.

KAREN RASBERRY It has only happened a handful of times, but sitting in the sunroom watching snowflakes fall makes me feel like I'm inside my very own giant snow globe. Favorite objects: A vintage New Orleans promotional poster by Continental Airlines. An oil painting purchased in Gatlinburg, Tennessee, in 1975 (a most unlikely place to find beach art). The navy-blue-and-white buffalo check sofa and the wool "tree of life" rug still make me happy after twenty-nine years. Surprisingly, a few of the furnishings I bought on a whim have become timeless.

KEYANNA BOWEN　My husband, Daniel, is a composer/pianist, and was gifted a 1900s Steinway piano from a family friend. Its body is old, the keys are worn, but when played, the beauty of its sound is endless—it's perfectly imperfect, just like our home.

LEIGH MULDROW I think for the library, my favorite memory has to be when I first pitched the idea of turning the dining room into a library to Ben and he told me to put that on the ten-year list. So I told the kids I thought it should be a library, and they started bringing books downstairs and telling Ben they were doing their homework in the library. It was so funny and sweet—and convincing. He built the library within six months!

LOUISE COSTER The portrait above the fireplace is Lady Emily Smyth, a family ancestor. Much of the furniture belonged to parents and grandparents who are no longer with us, but it has been restored or reupholstered by us and will hopefully be enjoyed by future generations.

DREW SCOTT   The theme of the artwork we have by the movie screen in the basement is anything to do with having a good time. The LUCKY neon sign used to hang in our Vegas house. It was custom-made as a nod to our dad, Jim, whose nickname was Lucky during his cowboy days. On the shelf opposite this sign, we display a few random things that just remind us of fun memories: a hand-painted sign from Honest Ed's in Toronto; a couple of retired, highly contentious cards from one of our favorite games, Codenames; and a homemade birthday party invitation.

TESSA FOLEY (ABOVE) This is where I started my business: sitting at an antique pine table that doubles as my desk, overlooking the trees in our backyard. This is where I experiment with textile combinations, gather inspiration, draw floor plans, and daydream. Where I manage orders and deadlines, pay bills, and send emails. I intentionally designed it to feel like a summer cottage on Nantucket, since that is the place where I feel most inspired and at peace.

SHELLIE WHITFIELD (OPPOSITE) With our lives being so chaotic, having my very own space full of sunlight and happy things allows me to breathe and create and remember who I am . . . which restores my soul. This space is where I take the idea of things that matter to people, and then through color, pattern, and texture, paint how they feel about them. It is truly where paint meets joy.

9

Kitchen

"I WOULD renovate this kitchen first thing if I were moving in here."

That was the singular criticism Mrs. Mary Lynn shared as she walked us through this house I had admired from the street my whole life. She had occupied it for a decade, during which time Hurricane Katrina shoved an ancient pecan tree through the roof and much of the first floor was flooded and thrashed by the wind and rain. In the aftermath, the Sheetrock, electrical, floors, and roof were all repaired and improved, but the tree wasn't big enough to reach the kitchen, so it remained unchanged aside from paint since the 1980s. It was a faceless, unremarkable kitchen with prefab white cabinets, light-gray laminate countertops, a stainless steel sink, a builder-grade white fridge and white stove, and baby-blue walls that seemed more frigid than cheerful. Some kitchens are greasy tragedies of linoleum and roach motels, cracking plexiglass backsplashes and fluorescent lights, but this was not one of them. She cooked often for her big family, but you would never know it. There were no recipes clipped from the newspaper under fridge magnets, or tomatoes ripening on the windowsill.

It was just a tidy room that smelled of dish soap. Generic, impersonal, and clean, with a popcorn ceiling. It was the sour note in the beautiful song of this house. I wanted warmth, connection, personality, love to come from it.

We renovated that kitchen first thing when we bought the house in September 2011, on a shoestring budget, between the hours of 5 p.m. and midnight.

With our incomes as an artist and a student minister, our renovation fund upon the purchase of our first home was $8,000. We resolved not to move in until the kitchen was complete; we would do the work ourselves, with what we had, and we would not go over budget. We kept the cabinet bases and replaced the doors, bought maple butcher-block countertops from IKEA, scraped the ceiling with a pumping bug sprayer and a putty knife, suspended mercury-glass pendant lights from pulleys in the ceiling that were hardwired to the sink wall because it saved money on moving the electrical. Ben built a custom cabinet around the stainless refrigerator we found used on Craigslist, and we stole a cast-iron kitchen sink Ben's mama had been saving in the barn since she found it in a yard sale in 1995. Before the subway tile craze began, we found it on closeout for sixty cents a square foot and bought all of it for our backsplash. We worked in the dark, by shop lights and extension cords, and our pants got tighter on our diet of drive-through burgers and fries for supper five nights a week. We taught ourselves how to renovate, to plumb, to build in six months, and by Easter Sunday we were pulling a ham out of the oven with our family crowded around the dinner table.

That first iteration of our kitchen was cute and frugal and it served us well for seven years. It was not expensive, but it photographed well. I cooked often, luxuriating in owning our own house with a proper kitchen, but we ate plenty of sandwiches too. There was music and kissing and supper parties, but there was also the day I found out I might have difficulty ever conceiving because of a decade-long illness and Ben held me close in the kitchen while I cried into his chest, muffling my sad wailing. It was the kitchen where I learned to make my mother's pecan pie, my friend Lily's famous cranberry granola, the spaghetti and meatballs I make for everyone's birthday. And eventually, it was where I made Helen's first bottle of formula and thanked God for a perfect, healthy baby girl. It was the kitchen I had when *Home Town* began, even as we honed our craft and learned what possibilities existed for

the many unique kitchens we were designing for our clients. As Helen learned to crawl on the heart pine floors, I began to notice the sag of the shelves that held the empty plastic tubs and lids she loved to stack. By fall 2018, our secondhand fridge's ice maker went out, and I thought, *I'd love to get a fridge that's a little bigger!* With Helen eating so many fresh fruits and vegetables, the refrigerator was always impossibly full. To pull the carrot salad out of the back meant dragging a tub of butter out onto the floor, but to have a larger fridge meant we'd need a larger fridge cabinet. To have a larger fridge cabinet meant the countertops would have to become a bit shorter. By January 2019, our cute kitchen knew the jig was up and was trying to quit before we could fire it. My secondhand oven would cut off midway through baking, and the back left eye on the stovetop was ornery, working only when the mood struck. The hot water in the kitchen stopped working and the faucet had calcium buildup that sent the water spraying askew, straight into the side wall of the sink, leaving us with wet shirts every time we washed a dish. For its death rattle, after a week of unending rain, a leak bubbled out of the ceiling over the kitchen sink that swelled and grew into a potbelly over twenty-four hours. By forty-eight hours, the Sheetrock had collapsed into the sink. In a room where so much water and heat happen, quality matters, so I prepared to build a kitchen that would last.

Ben chose rift-sawn white oak for our cabinets, a nod to our home's craftsman architecture. I designed the upper drawers to step out and the bases to step back, giving us more counter space and room to stand without a toe kick. I wanted the cabinets to feel like built-in furniture, to feel solid. Forever. We kept the layout exactly as it was, only the materials became stronger and better. The honed-quartz countertops that look like limestone; American-made appliances that were built by skilled craftspeople in Pennsylvania, Tennessee, and Ohio; and the handcrafted mahogany kitchen table with turned legs built by Ben all gave our kitchen a visual moment of enduring style that finally suited the architecture of a century-old home. It was no longer unremarkable or generic, cute, or (unfortunately!) frugal. It cost us, but investing in the houses that have seen Black Friday and the Second World War seems a worthy investment in preserving history.

For my first Mother's Day with the final iteration of our kitchen, Ben gave me a set of handmade copper pots from my friend Cat Bude's shop in France. While I love the look of them hanging in a kitchen, I loved even more the

prospect of actually cooking with them. Rather than read the instructions, I drizzled olive oil into the bottom of one and poured popcorn kernels in to make a snack. As the pot heated up and the popcorn began thumping around, I panicked as I watched the tin inside dimple and pock angrily where every grain of salt stuck: it was melting. I snapped off the gas eye and rushed to the sink to cool it down, then ran to the trash to rifle through it in search of the leaflet "Caring for Your Copper Cookware." One side was in French, the other in English, and I had tears in my eyes as I emailed Cat to ask if I had ruined my biggest, fanciest pot. After inspecting my photos, she assured me it was fine—I had taken it off just in time. I now consider myself an expert simply because I know that you can only cook liquids in copper cookware, like, say, spaghetti sauce and meatballs.

Of all the rooms in our home, the kitchen feels the most like it belongs to our friends. When we host supper, while I'm in a frenzied dash from pantry to range, trash to sink, our friends and brothers and parents find themselves pulled in. Though there is no place to sit, and it is the hottest room in the house in the middle of meal preparation, everyone is there: the kids underfoot, the adults mid-conversation as we intuitively dance around each other in the hunt for this bowl or that vinegar, the sizzling skillet and the boiling pot adding their noisy chatter, the smells of garlic or bacon making our mouths water. After we've eaten and lingered over stories, it is our friends who feel comfortable opening every drawer in search of the Pyrex for leftovers, the dishwashing liquid, the tinfoil. My best friend, Mallorie, knows my kitchen the way I know hers, where the kids' cups and the coffee mugs are, where the spatulas and knives go from the dishwasher, because we've spent so many years spreading butter on bread together. Our kitchen comes alive and welcomes everyone in with the fervor and warmth of a mother welcoming her kids home after a long separation. She is grand now, if a bit small, pulling us all together into her hug as we await the meal or say good-bye at the end of the night. They say the kitchen is the heart of the home, but I'd specify: the bosom. ✦

> Of all the rooms in our home, the kitchen feels the most like it belongs to our friends.

ANTHONY D'ARGENZIO Renovating and decorating with antiques and vintage items is an important element in all of my designs. One of my most special finds was the primitive antique cupboard we repurposed for the kitchen sink base. I also love the antique doors that were reclaimed from an old library—making for a movable wall for the primary suite.

CAROLINE BURKS Livi took her first wobbly, independent steps across the wood floor in our kitchen. She had on socks and the floors are so smooth that she didn't make it far, but those steps signaled the end of her babyhood, and I still think about it some nights now when I'm making dinner or doing dishes and she's running circles through the house.

Home Town, Season 2

THE BURKS HOUSE

In the kitchen, we started from scratch
and let the fireplace brick discovery lead us down a
textural, warm path to a brick kitchen as well.

—*ERIN*

CAT BUDE What we call the front kitchen (the kitchen comprises two rooms in a T shape) is decorated both with objects found on the farm and with flea market finds. Because of my business, we are at the markets weekly, and have a long history of friendships in the antiques world. I feel like every piece of furniture, every item and artwork, has a meaning and a memory—where we found it, how we chose to use it—from the nineteenth-century butcher's counter that we use as our main prep counter, to the antique printer's cabinet that I now use to hold all of my culinary tools and utensils.

———————

Home Town, Season 3

THE JAMES HOUSE

Getting to know the Jameses before we renovated their home,
I learned how important Emily's Mexican heritage is to her—the style, the
colors, the food, and the culture all became touchstones in the
design process, where we are always trying to find the common threads
between what the house gives us (architecture) and who the homeowners
are (personality). The printed vinyl backsplash was a budget-friendly
nod to painted Mexican tile. I've now had two opportunities to
design craftsman homes with Mexican-inspired design moments, and this
was the first and most subtle—keeping things youthful, modern,
and airy, like the family moving into it.

—ERIN

ALY SMITH   I think every day that I cook in my kitchen is a new favorite memory. Just the mundane things like cooking and cleaning, waving out my kitchen window to the Nowells as they drive by, listening to my favorite playlist as I wait for Jordan to get home from work while the pups are at my feet hoping that I'll drop something for them to grab.

EMILY SAXTON This is the room where everyone ends up gathering no matter what. We pile into the bay window breakfast nook, sit on the stools by the island, and this room is special because it's where we eat our food and make our food. Most nights we make dinner together and play fun music on the HomePod, and we dance while we cook. This started with just my husband and me dancing together while we tag-teamed dinner and debriefed about our days; then we added our puppy and now our baby girl to our nightly dance party.

ERICA SWAGLER The kitchen is one of the most hardworking rooms in the house, and one of the smallest, I'll add. From meal prep and dinners to craft projects with the kids at the table, singing "Happy Birthday" while gathered—so many happy occasions. There have been countless discussions (fun and serious) while gathered as a family and a couple around the table in this space.

LAUREN LIESS All the kitchen dancing happens in here. I love making big ole meals and dancing with my family as we cook and clean.

JENNIFER FAITH My favorite room is the kitchen. My favorite memories involve the whole family hanging out in there while I cook, or cooking alongside my son. I love dogs at my feet while I cook or bake. I love hanging out at the banquette with my family or playing games.

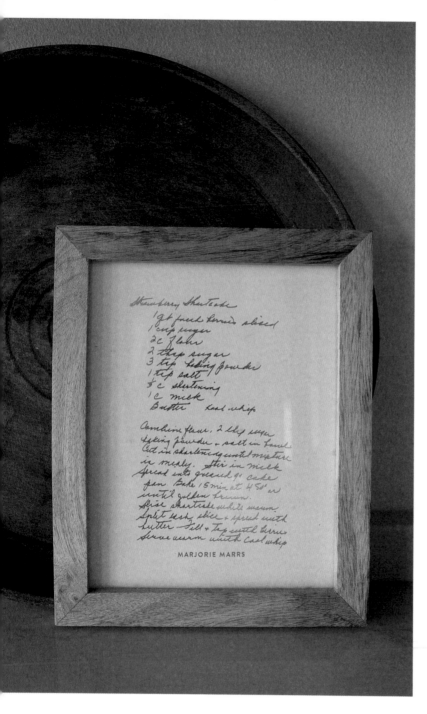

Strawberry Shortcake
  1 qt fresh berries sliced
  1 cup sugar
  2 c Flour
  2 tbsp sugar
  3 tsp baking powder
  1 tsp salt
  ⅓ c shortening
  1 c milk
  Butter   Cool whip

Combine flour, 2 tbsp sugar
baking powder + salt in bowl
Cut in shortening until mixture
is mealy. Stir in milk
Spread into greased 9" cake
pan. Bake 15 min at 450° or
until golden brown.
Slice shortcake while warm
Split each slice & spread with
butter—Fill & top with berries
Serve warm with Cool whip

MARJORIE MARRS

JENNY MARRS The gold-foiled print of Grandma Marrs's strawberry shortcake recipe is one of my most beloved possessions. It represents all of the lessons we learned from her while in the kitchen together, the place she felt most at home. She loved preparing meals for her family and hospitality was her love language. Every time I glance over while stirring a pot of soup on the stove and glimpse her handwriting framed next to me, I smile.

KAREN RASBERRY The day I finally filled my mother-in-law's shoes and made the perfect pan of dressing for Thanksgiving is my best kitchen memory. And of course all the casual entertaining we've done over the years. The kitchen is everybody's favorite gathering place.

KAREN RASBERRY My most prized objects in the kitchen are all the artwork done by Erin, but especially the one of my sister Phyllis and me wearing bikinis on Biloxi Beach, Mississippi. It's named *The Summer of '76*.

KEYANNA BOWEN The kitchen was the first space I updated and my first time tackling a home (rental) renovation. Even though it wasn't a major remodel, I knew I would need a helping hand, so I called on my dad for help. He's a hobby carpenter, and while growing up I watched him build and renovate spaces in our family home. Working alongside him to make updates to my kitchen is a father-daughter moment I will never forget and will cherish forever.

254

LAUREN NAPIER It always smells like coffee or cinnamon raisin bread in the kitchen. All of the appliances have tiny handprints from Nell on them, and it hurts my heart to wipe them away. It gets the best light around lunchtime, and it's the warmest room in our house. So when the weather is freezing, you can find us gathered in the kitchen.

LAYLA QUILICHINI-ROVIRA Besides all the memories, if we ever moved I would miss the love this home has given to us; she feels like a big hug to me. Because of its size and floor plan, it moves us closer together. It's so good for spending time together.

LINDA CARSON The kitchen, with its dark, heavy beams and antiqued cabinetry, holds memories of creating favorite meals and special moments baking cookies with our grandchildren.

——————

Home Town, Season 1
THE CARSON HOUSE

The Carsons gave us so much creative freedom to really lean into their past life in France. They once lived in a 1600s château with a moat on the French-Belgian border but were moving into this vanilla postwar cottage that lacked personality. I felt enormous pressure to make this move back stateside worth it for them! It was an example of a total transformation of a house using its bones but changing its identity in every way to become historic, Provençal, a patina of history applied to a relatively modern home. The kitchen floors were a steal—inexpensive porcelain tile in two colors but inspired by Cat Bude's 1640 kitchen, which you will also find in this book. Back then, Cat was an inspiration to me, and now I'm lucky to count her as a friend.

—ERIN

RENA REGISTER I love the custom-built table from Ben Napier accompanied by the chairs that were my grandfather and grandmother's. I also love that the original pantry is still here! That pantry held many canned goods that my family gathered from the garden. One of those gardens is actually where my house sits today. I've given canning a try and canned tomatoes and pepper jelly from my own little garden. I'm also fond of the old herb and spice chart that's on my shelf. The sink in the kitchen is original to the house. I'm not certain if babies were bathed in it, but I have many memories of my grandmother standing there washing dishes, cutting vegetables, and preparing meals. On the right side of the sink was the old refrigerator that is now on my porch. I remember it was filled with everything good. I would sometimes spend the night with her and she would pull the bacon out and cook it till it was nearly burnt. She would also fix us a bowl of Cream of Wheat topped with a fried egg. She always drank a cup of hot water that she cooked on a small gas stove in the kitchen. I always got a cup too, and I managed to take a couple of sips just to be like her.

PATTI WAGNER   When I think of our kitchen, I think of little footsteps running around the island while we cook and pick up. Memories of date night meals prepared by Brian. After we tuck the kiddos into bed, Brian makes these delicious meals and we have a romantic dinner with just us two.

TESSA FOLEY My favorite objects are my antique ironstone pitchers and platters. I discovered white ironstone at a small neighborhood antique shop when we lived in our first home. It was an inexpensive and easy way to add some old charm to our newly built home, so my collection grew quickly. When we moved into our current home sixteen years ago, my mum gave me a collection of ironstone pitchers she'd been saving, which are now displayed on my open shelves and in our hutch in the dining room. I use them for flowers, to hold wooden spoons, and for table settings.

We hosted our first Thanksgiving for family in this home and that felt like a huge entertaining victory. I made my first turkey in this kitchen—which was a bit of a disaster because it wasn't fully thawed on the morning of Thanksgiving. I've hosted every year since then and have switched to fresh turkeys. I spend so much time in this space, cooking and baking, that I have so many memories that I treasure: making Christmas cookies with Charlie, attempting multiple cider doughnut recipes, surprising my boys with homemade soft pretzels after school, cooking through every one of Ina Garten's cookbooks, and listening to Jimmy turn up the music and sing while he does the dishes every night. I mastered homemade pie crust in this kitchen, made dinners for friends who just had babies and others coping through a hard time. I've packed up class treats and swim-meet bake sale items and made my famous chocolate cake for every birthday celebration. Hard to pick just one memory...

VICTORIA FORD   Would we miss our kitchen if we ever moved? Sure. But we would miss this period of time in our lives when we were picking out colors for it more. This house is the story of our life at this time and our routine. I would miss that feeling of home and the creation of place that I could only get here.

We had this "serve 'em up" kitchen cabinet mounted to our ceiling above a peninsula, and my husband and I pulled it down within a day of living here. It let this magical amount of light into our kitchen and just felt a bit like time stopped in the best way.

10

Back Porch

THIS WAS the end. The final renovation to our beloved cottage, the latecomer in snapshots of our life in this house. When we first moved in, thankful to have a yard, adding a back porch was a "someday" task we would complete. We had steps up to the laundry room door off the kitchen and some flagstone pavers in the grass where Ben set up his grill. The backyard was for our dogs, Baker and Chevy, or for shooting basketball in the garage driveway, but it was not yet the romantic, twinkling plein air space where we would eventually host dinners for friends. On *Home Town* we often say the back porch is for the introverts, while the front porch is for the extroverts, a social event. We know this from experience, that a front porch life means watching and visiting, noticing when the elderly neighbor seems to be losing some of their dexterity, when one day a baby is no longer in a stroller but now stumbling alongside his parents. We had the front porch, and our life then was a front porch kind of life without the need for privacy or more room for children to play. Our urgent desire for a back porch came with the advent of Helen walking. Children need dirt and sun and water to blossom like dandelions, to make messes and mud pies. Ben chose mahogany for the decking, and I wanted cream-painted X-railing with wide steps and shallow risers, easy for little ones to climb, so we built it at the end of our kitchen renovation in spring 2019. Ben built a swing set from heart pine in the backyard and strung party lights from the house to the porch's top rail.

In March, the days in Mississippi are brisk, windy, and sun-drenched. The pollen begins to collect like the sawdust in Ben's woodshop, thick and unrelenting by the end of the month, but for a few bright weeks it is the perfect time to be outdoors in the Deep South. Our first weeks of the COVID quarantine were premature: Mississippi didn't see many official cases until late 2020, but we were following the rules and keeping ourselves at home, thankful to live in rural America, where even our cities have breathing room and you can take a long walk without coming closer than thirty yards to another living person. Our backyard became our most used space in these months.

After toting Helen down from her crib at 7 a.m., we would walk out onto our back porch in the shade of the Japanese magnolia tree and the cherry-colored umbrella that skewers the dinner table. I would buckle Helen into her high chair on the porch and give her toasted waffles and raspberries and milk, while we had toast and jam and coffee in our pajamas (or underwear, or robes, but certainly never real clothes). Music was always playing, and that spring it was a band called Caamp that was the soundtrack to our life. To even type the name of that band makes my heart feel a tenderness for that time when we were safe at home together on that back porch with no work to go to for so many weeks, our only job to marvel at our growing baby.

It was bittersweet, the bliss of togetherness tempered by the worry about the pandemic and our finances if the show were to shut down for many months. We were in a happy and sugar-sweet kind of purgatory without knowing what our life would look like a week, a month from then. I only knew I would be cooking lunch and then dinner from scratch and we would eat every meal on the back porch between anxious, masked, hurried visits to the grocery store, where people were rationing like wartime. My agenda was cleared and the days stretched out in front of us: cooking, singing, walking, playing with Helen, waiting for normal life to resume, wishing we never had to leave her at home again. We brought the laptop to the porch dinner table

She would snuggle against him as he
lay by the dinner table and get comfortable there,
moving his fur, like a flokati rug, around her
fingers and whispering, "I love Baker."

during Helen's nap one day to make a spread-sheet of our nonnegotiable expenses and how long we could make it without working, if it came to that. I ate fresh sweet strawberries and good cheese while a breeze that smelled like the dryer vent blew through the trees. That was the paradox of quarantine: dread and delight, intermingled.

One Christmas a couple years prior, Ben had surprised me with a bulk order of canvases for painting—dozens of them, in every size—optimistic about my time and ambition to make new art even with a baby and the show consuming my life. Two years later they sat still shrink-wrapped in my art studio downtown, watching me accusingly as I dabbled in watercolors and answered emails. By March 2020, I had mostly forgotten them until Helen suddenly showed an interest in the kiddie temperas I had gotten for her, and I brought home an armload of them. I spread out a drop cloth on the back porch and propped a four-foot-tall canvas against the railing, then set out her brushes and paints and watched as our two-year-old, stripped down to her diaper and rainboots, smeared and splashed the colors in wild lines and blobs. The colors and forms without meditation were so full of curiosity and beauty, it made my eyes water. After a few minutes, I set the canvas aside to dry in the sun. Every day for many weeks I would bring that same canvas to the drop cloth and my near-naked girl would add to her master-piece, until one day it was a finished, layered story about what happens when green meets yellow and red and black. It was precious to me, our baby's first expressions with so much color and vibrancy during a bleak and troubled time in history.

By the end of the summer we were back to work filming *Home Town*, and our idle week-days on the back porch were gone. On Saturdays, we dragged a blue plastic swimming pool onto the porch for Helen to splash in after painting. This was around the time she fell in love with Baker, our only remaining dog, an eleven-year-old Great Pyrenees. He moved gingerly with arthritic hips, the best energy level for a curious toddler. She would snuggle against him as he lay by the dinner table and get comfortable there, moving his fur, like a flokati rug, around her fingers and whispering, "I love Baker." She would place her soft rolling unicorn toy atop his head as he sat, content and bewildered, proud of the hat she'd made.

In May 2021, I was nine months pregnant and waiting for Mae to arrive at any time. We had leave from work for a few months and the back porch was our playground again most days, if Ben and Helen weren't off swimming in a big pool somewhere, since Helen had become adept at swimming like a fish in the year since COVID began. I felt like overripe fruit, my skin tight and my back aching from the extra weight I was carrying. My denim shorts were unable to button, so I sat with my feet in the kiddie pool on the porch while Helen and I shared Popsicles and listened to the music from *Bluey*, a phenomenon that had recently consumed our family. Baker was having trouble walking now, and we were making him comfortable. We scratched his head and back, giving him bites of our grilled foods and a lick from the last of the ice cream cups. There were no more trips around the block with him by the time Mae was born, and a month later, after only a few naps together on the back porch with our newborn, Baker passed away. It was a very hard lesson in grief for Helen, who didn't understand how permanent and imminent death was, something we're still grappling with explaining to her a year later. We saw it coming for many months, but she thought he might live forever, that they would be lying in the grass together watching the shapes in the clouds even when she was a mommy to her own babies someday.

Her heartbreak waxed and waned. Some days she would not mention Baker, her first love. But some overtired nights, he was the only balm that could soothe her wailing, sleepy fits. "If Baker was here, everything would be okay! Everything would go back to normal!" I'm unsure if normal meant the time when we had a dog or before there was an attention-stealing baby sister, but it stung, nonetheless. I felt immobilized in those moments, hurt that she felt we had turned away from her and toward Mae during her first heartbreak, and also like a puppy might heal the break but be too much to care for with a new baby in our arms. Once Mae was nine months old, we felt ready to commit to another dog and surprised Helen with a fluffy Great Pyrenees puppy. She snuggled her face into the fur around his neck and whispered, "You came back, Baker." And so another Baker is on the porch again, but this time he is young and teething and eating the girls' bicycle tires in the shade of the oak trees, learning how to walk on a leash, learning how to be a guardian to two little girls who believe he will keep them safe as long as he is alive. Our back porch feels like it is shrinking with two grown-ups, two kids, and one very big and busy dog sharing the four hundred square feet. It's a party all the time, but the right kind for an introvert, where I know everyone at the party and we're all in our pajamas when we arrive. ✪

EMILY SAXTON We are outside people, so we love this space and sit out here often. There are a few months in Mississippi that are so perfect weather-wise that we just have to sit and enjoy as many meals outside as we can. During COVID stay-home-order season, we felt trapped and alone, but bringing meals outside to enjoy on our table and sitting here on our bench together felt peaceful and was a companion to us during a lonely season. The perfect spot to enjoy coffee in the morning. The perfect spot to enjoy a fire in the fire pit when the cooler weather comes around. We celebrated our fifth and sixth wedding anniversaries out here when we couldn't go anywhere, and they have been our favorites so far. The twinkle lights strung above give a nod to the magical ones that line our sweet little downtown in Laurel.

LAUREN LIESS I love hanging out here after a full day of planting in my garden and looking at our handiwork. Sometimes it'll rain, and I just love being out here cuddled up with my husband. (There's a sofa on the other side.)

LAYLA QUILICHINI-ROVIRA

JENNIFER FAITH Our yard is a favorite spot to hang out in in the evenings, with the string lights lit. The garden is a spot I'm really proud of. My husband built the rock garden beds for me for my birthday, and I love them even more because he made them. I love working in the vegetable beds with my dogs running around playing.

JENNIFER WEBER When I was growing up, my best friend, Liz, had a wonderful screened porch on her house. I have sweet memories of everything from playing Barbies and eating summer lunches to senior class parties there. As soon as we had the chance, we added our take on that porch to our home. I love fall afternoons with a fire in the fireplace and football on the TV on the porch, with a view of grandchildren playing in the backyard.

MALLORIE RASBERRY   My mind can't even begin to imagine that we would ever leave this house. I've already grown old with this house. I'm a little embarrassed to admit I've already planned our girls' wedding receptions in the side yard—*Father of the Bride* style.

IN THE FAMILY

Mallorie and Jim's house

Mallorie and Jim's house feels like our other home.
We spend so much time here since my best friend, Mallorie,
married my first cousin Jim, who is one of Ben's
best friends, and they are our business partners. Our girls are
cousins and best friends, but also: they have a pool.

—*ERIN*

Home Town, Season 4

THE REGISTER HOUSE

Tiny little houses are the fan favorites of *Home Town,*
and I think it's because many of us have had this fantasy of life
pared down, where we pick vegetables from a garden in the
backyard, we do with less, in an idyllic little cottage in the country.
Rena's home was a perfect candidate for telling that story and
using a truly Americana color palette that felt at home in a grove of
pecan trees. It is practical, friendly, and bursting with personality,
all words I would use to describe Rena as well.

—ERIN

RENA REGISTER (ABOVE) The side porch holds the original refrigerator that was in the house. Showing its age with rust, but it still runs. My side porch is probably my favorite space. I can look over to see my mom's house and even watch to make sure she's okay when she's working in her flowerbeds. I also have views of the sunrise and the sunset. I sometimes sit alone or with my pup, Champ, and think about when I was a little girl running around on the property. The pecan trees are magical year-round. They offer tons of shade in the summer and beautiful colors in the fall. I love having friends over to sit and chat on the porch. And I love when my family comes over (particularly my nieces and nephews) and they help themselves to a cold drink from the old fridge that sits on the porch.

SANDRA M. CAVALLO We have countless memories and are still making memories today. We really enjoy entertaining, whether it's birthday dinners on the covered porch or big get-togethers on our deck off the kitchen. Outside spaces when you live in a beach community create another dimension to our home and special memories.

Acknowledgments

There are people in my life who made this book possible, who made it sing:

Ben, for building a life and a family and a history with me in our first house, for making me a mother to the girls who made our family complete.

My parents, for establishing the feeling of home and what it should be when I was a child. It was safety, love, creativity, and a lot of raisin bran and Eggos (which is also love). Thank you, Mama, for the books and stories you've written that inspired me to write too.

Mallorie Rasberry, for naming this book when my brain was wrung out and couldn't find the words, and who will always have the extra key to my house.

Aly Smith and Emily Nowell, my dear friends, who read this as I went along and encouraged what was special and good about it.

Laura Jones, my right hand and art director, thank you for your creative mind and being my second set of eyes, hands, and feet.

Brooke Davis-Jefcoat, who has been behind the camera documenting my life since my wedding. I wouldn't trust anyone else to help me tell these stories.

Kim Perel, my agent, who always believes in the stories I write.

Clay Hunt, our manager, who pushes me to dream bigger every year.

Misty Moore, who loves our babies when I have to leave them to work and write. Our world would fall apart without you. Because you're there, I can take the time to record our family's history in this short, precious season of child-rearing.

The editorial team at Simon & Schuster, thank you for trusting my vision for this unusual book, for understanding and supporting the why and the how of it.

The friends and family who've visited our home and gave me the stories to tell.

My contributors from all over the world who took the time to write thoughtfully about their homes, who trusted me when I asked them to photograph it in its unkempt and blessedly normal state, thank you for sharing your lives and homes with the reader, who will no doubt see a reflection of themselves in it.

Survey

When I invited real-life friends, Instagram friends, former clients, and family to contribute to this book and share their homes, I sent them this short list of questions to capture their stories about the rooms they photographed. I present the questions to you here to help you dig deep thinking about what makes your home yours, what makes it important, even in the total disarray of living: dirty laundry and dishes and scattered toys and unfinished renovations. It is still worthy of remembering.

NAME: _____

CITY, STATE: _____

PROFESSION: _____

HOME DESIGNED BY: _____

WHY DID YOU KNOW THIS HOUSE WAS THE ONE? WHAT DREW YOU TO IT?

_____

_____

_____

_____

_____

_____

_____

_____

_____

WHAT IS YOUR FAVORITE MEMORY FROM EACH OF THE ROOMS IN YOUR HOUSE?

FRONT PORCH: _____

_____

_____

_____

ENTRY: _____

_____

_____

_____

LIVING ROOM: _____

_____

_____

_____

DINING ROOM: _____

_____

_____

_____

BEDROOM: _____

_____

_____

_____

GUEST ROOM(S): _____

_____

_____

_____

BATHROOM: _____

_____

_____

_____

OFFICE / EXTRA ROOM(S): _____

_____

_____

_____

KITCHEN: _____

_____

_____

_____

BACK PORCH: _____

_____

_____

_____

TELL ME A STORY ABOUT SOME OF THE OBJECTS IN THESE ROOMS THAT ARE MEANINGFUL TO YOU:

_____

_____

_____

_____

_____

_____

_____

_____

DESCRIBE YOUR HOME IN THREE WORDS: _____

_____

IF YOU WERE TO MOVE, WHAT WOULD YOU MISS MOST ABOUT THIS HOUSE?

_____

_____

_____

_____

_____

_____

About the Author

Erin Napier is an artist, author, designer, and entrepreneur with a fine-arts degree who started her career in corporate graphic design before founding her own international stationery company, Lucky Luxe. She is also a founding co-owner of Laurel Mercantile Co. and Scotsman Co.

Six days after meeting in college, Erin and Ben decided they would marry, and they've been inseparable ever since, working side by side in every venture. Their passion for small-town revitalization and American craftsmanship is evident in their stores, Laurel Mercantile Co., Scotsman Co., and the Scent Library, where they design and manufacture heirloom wares and durable goods made exclusively in the United States. They live in Laurel, Mississippi, with their two daughters, Helen and Mae, where they restore homes on HGTV's *Home Town*.